Make Yourself

Magic

Also by Jaclyn Lanae

The Me I Was

Make Yourself

Magic

Actionable steps to help you manifest a life you *love.*

Jaclyn Lanae

Published in 2018
Shelter 50 Publishing Collective
Rapid City, South Dakota, USA

For commercial purposes please contact:
Shelter50publishingcollective@gmail.com
www.Shelter50PublishingCollective.com

Printed and bound in the United States of America

First edition, 2018

Book cover design by Kim Lathe
www.kimlathe.com

ISBN 978-0-9862495-9-4

In deep and humble gratitude to all my teachers…

Contents:

Authors Note:

This is not the book I intended to write. After publishing my first book - a memoir titled *The Me I Was* - I was sure I'd write fiction. Because, as it turns out, sometimes telling the truth is hard. Alas, a writer is at the whim of her muse.

At its core, this book is one of ideas - or, rather, a collection of things I've learned and used to help me create the life I love, the life I'm living. These are meant to be actionable tools to support you in creating the life you want - and finding deep, lasting, happiness. YOUR happiness, however that looks for you. By its very nature, however, manifestation is - for me - inextricably linked with spirituality and while this is not necessarily a spiritual text, there will be references here and there to my own philosophy. It is utterly and completely unnecessary for you to adopt these belief systems in order to implement the suggestions I present here.

Additionally, while it most certainly flies in the face of convention - and proper writing rules - you will find that I often refer to God and dare to do so with the lower case 'g'. This is not in any way an effort to disrespect or devalue God (capital G), but instead a way for me to represent a universal god-type force. It is not my intention to offend or alienate, but instead to convey a more widely inclusive way of thinking about god.

It is also important to me to offer these ideas with full disclosure; while I have achieved tremendous success in my personal and professional life, I am in no way a licensed life coach, counselor, spiritual leader, or anything of the sort. I am simply a woman who has lived through a unique set of circumstances (as we all have) that led me to these ideas and conclusions. And I'm not perfect. Not by a long shot. My great hope with this work is that in sharing my own experiences I can illuminate one of many possible paths toward the life of your dreams, and help you love the life you're living.

As always, I encourage you to take from this text that which truly resonates with you, that which you believe will work for you, and leave the rest behind.

Incidentally, if you do feel a connection to my way of thinking about spirituality and the human condition, please visit my website, and subscribe to my blog at www.AuthorJaclynLanae.com

If you would like to read about the life I led that brought me to this place, I encourage you to enjoy my first book; The Me I Was, also available on my website.

Best wishes to you and may your journey be filled with abundance, joy, love, and magic.

Special thanks to Deb, Mary, and Melanie for your incredible wisdom… and to Kim Lathe for your incredible design talents.

Introduction

While, as previously mentioned, adopting my personal belief system is in no way essential to mastering manifestation as it is laid out in this work, an awareness of the perspective from which I come will be valuable as we embark on this journey together.

First and foremost, I think of god as a force of energy. Or, perhaps more accurately, as *the collective* energy of everything. Everything. Rocks have energy, water has energy, light has energy, wood has energy, even thoughts and feelings have an energy, a vibration. Personally, I believe that as energy beings, we are *all* elements of god and therefore we - all energy beings taken together – are god.

I also believe that we have the power to adjust our own energy and that our bodies - physical, mental, and spiritual - function as something akin to a tuning fork; vibrating at a certain frequency to draw into our lives the people, things, and circumstances that exist at a similar vibration. This is the crux of my belief about manifestation; by managing our energy, our 'magnets', we can create lives we love living.

Secondly, I believe at the soul-level, we are all seeking to most perfectly "tune-in" to our personal god-self frequency and share that version of ourselves with the world. The sweet little cherry on top is that in the effort to ever more perfectly connect to our god-selves, we also begin to vibrate more and more as pure, soul-self energy, and in doing so, we can more easily manifest the lives we want; the lives our soul-selves want.

I believe we "tune-in" to ourselves by loving as deeply as possible. Particularly, loving *ourselves*. I am not god, but god is me. And you. And us all. (More on self-love later. Lots more.)

Thirdly, I think of our minds as computers (albeit incredibly complex systems that we only barely understand). They are slaves to our habits, environment, education, self-talk, and so on. I believe we can use the power of our minds to "tune in" to our soul-selves & adjust our frequency, influencing our vibration, our energy, our magnet. Directing our personal energy to match as closely as possible the vibration in which we want to exist as the self and reality we most desire is, for me, the true art of making ourselves magic.

Whether conscious or unconscious we are always creating, magnet-ing. We get to choose what we attract. By monitoring and guiding the *conscious* mind, we can help to manage and even train our *subconscious* to feed us 'good'.

This premise is the foundation of the following work; a text devoted to ways we can help program our subconscious to influence us in a positive way, and adjust our current vibration or frequency to draw to ourselves that which we truly want to manifest in our lives.

Finally, THE key... the single most important thing I will say in this work and to anyone who asks about my life and belief system is summed up in these three words; LOVE YOURSELF MORE.

I believe we live our best life by focusing on ourselves – on loving ourselves; thereby more deeply loving god and providing a better, more purely god-soul self to give to others.

There is nothing, in my experience or in the education I've received from other masters, that more quickly or more deeply connects you to the essence of who you really are, your soul self, the god that lives within you... than loving yourself. Truly, deeply, honestly loving yourself. Not your ego-self; the one that wants to judge and compare, to be "better than"… But your true self; who you really are as a spirit being on a soul-level.

First and last, again and again, no matter the question or the problem the simple answer is always: LOVE YOURSELF MORE. Love the way you think, the way you eat, the way you talk to yourself, the way you laugh, the way you learn, the way you tell stories, the way you believe, the way you see the world, the way you connect to god, the way you listen to the universe, the way you cook, the way you treat people, *the way you treat YOURSELF*. Love yourself – your god-force-self – so you can give yourself what you really want, what your soul-self wants, and you will draw to you all you want and need, and more. As if by magic.

The first step, then, is to tune into yourself, as you are right now, and raise your "base level" vibration.

1

Clean Physical Self

Your best self is your best self. By that, I mean that while (I imagine) it is possible to become a master manifest-er while living life in almost any way, the whole process is much easier when you are living as your best self. It's easier to feel good when you feel good. It's easier to be optimistic, hopeful, and happy when your body feels good, when your 'container', your tuning fork, is clean.

And don't we all want more "feel good" in our lives anyway?

A tuning fork works best when free of dirt and grime, sound and light vibrate best through clear air and water, and I believe you will find your success in manifesting nearly anything and everything your heart desires will be dramatically improved by living a "clean" life. A healthier you will find it easier to be positive, happy, motivated, patient, encouraging, and so on which will help you naturally "vibrate higher" and attract more 'good', more easily. This also makes you a better partner, a better lover, a better mother, a better employee, a better friend, and on and on and on.

Living a clean life *is* loving yourself; not only who you are in your heart, but also your physical self in the choices you make for your body every day. After all, those seemingly small daily decisions ultimately define us. The things in our lives we prioritize are the things that really matter to us. Otherwise, we'd do other things. So, prioritize yourself – the way you care for, the way you LOVE your body. Make choices you'll be proud you made.

That said, we are human and I believe that state of being in itself is a gift. The pursuit of perfection in ourselves and in our lives is a quest doomed to failure. Perfect isn't real. And often the pressure to achieve a state of perfect - and the fear that we will fail - keeps us from starting at all. Or finishing. Particularly when we've got some idea of a perfect body, a perfect diet, a perfect gym routine.

All of life is a gift. Have a piece of pie once in awhile. But just once in a while.

The following suggestions need not be implemented in any particular order. In fact, I suggest finding one actionable point which excites you, for which you have some personal energy, and starting there. For instance, if the idea of exercise makes you want to pull the covers over your head, but the idea of learning some new recipes makes your mouth water, consider starting with revising your relationship with food. Or perhaps the idea of committing to 5 minutes of stillness every day is appealing. Or spending 10 minutes stretching. Whatever it is, pick a starting point and just start. It really is that simple.

Start small - and celebrate the small victories. Telling yourself you will go to the gym five hours a week, eat a vegetarian diet, drink only water and tea, and begin meditating... on Monday... is really setting yourself up for failure. Tell yourself you will add a serving of leafy greens to six of your weekday meals. Then give yourself a pat on the back or a tangible reward when you follow through. But don't give yourself a cheesecake.

Food

Growing up, my mother worked hard to instill very healthy food habits in my sister and I. We had a salad with every meal, rarely ate fried foods, and were allowed almost no sugar. When I discovered peanut-butter-and-chocolate candy in High School, I set about an unspoken mission to undo all my mother's teachings. I really mastered the effort in college. By my sophomore year, I felt fat, insecure, lazy and brinking on depression. Well after college I finally drifted back to my roots and began cooking for myself again. The difference was shocking. Eventually I grasped what my mother had been trying to tell me all along; what you put in your mouth matters, and it changed my whole relationship with food.

Eat Your Veggies

Food is a fundamental building block of life. It has energy of its own and when you consume the food, you consume its energy. There are enough books on the topics of food and nutrition to fill your local library - perhaps several times over - so I will not delve into the science here. Personally, I have found that keeping it simple is the easiest approach; eat mindfully, food that is as close as possible to the way it came from the earth. At first, don't worry about calories, or portion size. Simply eat slowly enough to truly enjoy your food and focus on consuming as many fruits and vegetables as possible.

Why fruits and vegetables? Because they come almost directly from the earth. Whereas animal products are somewhat removed from the earth first because the animals themselves consume vegetation and process it before we ever get to it, (sometimes even the 'vegetation' fed to the animals is processed before *they* consume it) and second because animal products also generally require some processing to be fit for grocery store shelves. Restaurants often process them even further. Vegetables and fruits are very literally the fruit of the earth. You could pull a fist full of spinach out of the ground and put it in your mouth. Though you'd probably find it quite gritty and a little wanting in flavor. But you could do it and it would be really good for your body.

When I am approached on the idea of healthy eating and adjusting food habits in general, the first thing I always suggest is ADDING something healthy and cutting down on the quantity of the other stuff. Feeling deprived is often one of the primary reasons people struggle to eat a healthier diet. Start by adding healthier foods to the meals you already eat - again, taking the time to eat mindfully. Just remember to cut down the portions of the other foods on your plate too. Eating MORE, even if it's 'healthy' won't help as much.

Begin by committing to consuming at least one fruit or vegetable with two of your daily meals. Work up to two or more at every meal, with the end goal of consuming almost exclusively vegetables, nuts, seeds, and fruits.

Are you freaking out a little? Don't panic. Take your time with the transition. Choose foods you will enjoy eating, and even preparing. Make time to prepare and eat at home. And pay attention to your body. You may find over time that you really do feel better, and that you actually prefer the taste of 'real' food. But don't force yourself into a too-strict regimen too fast or you'll feel like you're on a diet, and you'll hate it and it won't stick. Eat what you want – just focus on adding more fresh fruits and veggies.

If eating "veggie" is somewhat foreign to you, don't obsess about preparation. Going from no-veggies to raw-only veggies might be too drastic. Do, however, pay attention to processing. Spinach from the farmers market is better than spinach from the store, and both are better than blanched, frozen spinach from the freezer section. Frozen is way better for your body than cream cheese and mayonnaise spinach dip. You get the idea. Eventually, you may prefer to eat your veggies closer to raw and less covered in cheese or dressings, but don't push it if you aren't ready.

At restaurants, consider eating like a vegetarian; order a vegetable dish as your main course, or add a vegetable to your meal and eat it first, before you eat the meat or bread or pasta.

If you choose to eat meat, really *choose* your meat. Animals processed for big brand-name meat providers are often treated quite poorly - even if they qualify to be labeled "organic". Whatever hormones and other junk are forced into those animals will likely turn up in their meat, and subsequently in your body. Take some time to search out a local chicken farmer or choose sustainably, wild caught fish products. Buffalo, for instance, are native to the United States and are FAR easier on the environment than cattle – so consider choosing sustainable, humanely harvested buffalo whenever possible. Finally, pay attention to how much meat you really consume. The human body does not need to eat bacon, sausage and eggs for breakfast, a burger for lunch, and steak for dinner. Just a few ounces of meat per week is generally sufficient.

Reconnect to your food - where it comes from and how it's handled - and you will reconnect to your body. (If you have questions or concerns about your nutritional needs, consult an expert.)

Back Off the Sugar

Sugar - particularly, processed, white sugar - is damaging to your body and, arguably, your mind. Either way, as we've acknowledged, the condition of your body impacts your mind. So, no matter, what, taking steps to eliminate sugar from your daily diet will likely both support your mastery of manifestation, and help you feel better in general. You may even lose weight and improve other measures of your overall health.

Again, if you are daunted by this prospect, start small. Perhaps instead of consuming several sodas every day, commit to consuming less; only before lunch, or only one per day, or only on weekends. In the meantime, find a replacement to help ease any mental anxiety you may have around the change. The brain is a computer, and it doesn't like to have its routine messed with. Particularly with a somewhat addictive substance like sugar. Substituting lemonade, or tea with honey may be a necessary bridge to lasting change.

And make it easy on yourself! If you want to feed yourself better things, don't keep cookies in the house. It just makes sense and it's a good start. Perhaps keep some salted nuts around instead of potato chips. If you really, REALLY want a cookie – have one! Just do it intentionally, with focus. Get in the car and drive yourself – or better yet, walk - to a local bakery, sit down and enjoy ONE really delicious cookie. Instead of an entire box of store-bought ones. Now be proud of yourself! You deserve a treat now and then. And you only had one. And you indulged yourself in a really intentional way – almost like you took yourself out on a date (more on this later). And you may have even supported a local business in the process. So you spent your money intentionally too. Well done!

Another of my favorite "tricks" to soothe my mind when it thinks it wants cheesecake is to health-i-fy it. For instance, when I want dessert, I buy several avocados, blend them with coconut oil, honey and mint extract, and pour the whole pitcher of thick, creamy, goodness into a pie tin. (Sometimes with a "healthy" homemade nut-crust, and sometimes with a store-bought graham cracker crust.) I might even mix in a cup of organic dark chocolate chips. I put it in the fridge and mix up some coconut cream "frosting". (Coco powder, coconut milk fat, and honey.) When I want dessert, I have avocados and dark chocolate, but it tastes like chocolate mint pie and that's all my mind needs to feel satisfied. There are whole cookbooks, blogs, websites, and prepared food companies devoted to this concept, so if you need ideas, I'd start there.

Over time, you may find you actually crave the "healthy" stuff. I do. Give me a salad and sweet potato fries with avocado pie over pizza and ice cream any day.

Moderate

Eating slowly is one of the ways experts suggest managing your weight because out-of-whack portions are a big reason people are overweight, feel sluggish, and generally less-than-good. Maintaining mindfulness while you eat may help you to reduce your portion sizes, and you may be surprised at how good it feels to just be full instead of stuffed. This may also help you re-set your body's awareness of how much food you actually need to feel satisfied and you may find you feel full with smaller portions.

Toxins

It goes without saying that polluting your body with drugs, alcohol, tobacco or other substances will not likely support you in creating the life of your dreams. Take a moment to understand your relationship with your toxin of choice, should you have one, and find the root reason for your use or abuse. What is it you are really getting out of cigarettes or alcohol or drugs? Time alone? A way to escape? A way to avoid boredom or hide from change? Maybe you are avoiding the work of creating the reality, the YOU, you really want?

The perception that your vice is helping you to feel better is a falsity. The chemical change that's happening in your brain isn't necessarily indicative of what's going on in your body.

Find a way to fill that desire and soothe your mind with something healthier for you. I always suggest something creative; art or exercise or music or reading… If you feel at the mercy of addiction, seek help. There are a lot more well qualified support people in the world than I - and I've seen the miracles they can work in people's lives. The sooner you do so, the more time you will have to live a happy, healthy, life you will love.

Like I said, I'm not perfect. I've struggled with tobacco use for years. But the closer I get to myself the easier it is to choose something else; something I'm proud to do / create / consume. And the more I do that the more I feel the profound difference in my body and mind. I'm so much more positive, energetic, patient, joyful, and quick-witted when I take good care of my body. I imagine that is the case for most of us.

Prioritizing veggies, cutting down on sugar, eating slowly, and eliminating toxins are great ways to embrace and even grow to love a healthier diet. Perhaps even a healthier you, and wouldn't that just be the coconut chocolate icing on the avocado mint pie.

Love what you put in to your body. Love the way you eat.

Exercise

Know Yourself

Years and years ago a friend of mine was embarking on a journey toward a healthier life and in her effort toward that goal, signed up for a 5am kickboxing class. When she invited me to join her one morning, I agreed, in the interest of supporting my friend and perhaps building some additional muscle. When we were paired together as the class was wrapping up, she held up pads while I punched, and asked whether I'd enjoyed it or not. "Yes," I panted between right hooks, "but I don't imagine I'll be coming again." I said it with a smile - at least as much of a smile as I could muster dripping with sweat at 5:45am, but I could see the shock pass across her face like headlights passing through a living room window. She made a well-meaning comment that I would only get out of it what I put in, to which I smiled again and nodded. And I never went back.

I wasn't embarrassed. I didn't feel like a quitter or a failure, and when I laughed about the experience to another friend she clarified my truth mid-giggle. "Yeah," she grinned, "you don't strike me as that *kind* of person. You strike me as more a 'gentle exercise' kind of person." She was right, and I had known that before I ever showed up at that 5am class - I just hadn't labeled it that way. I'm not at all unhappy that I attended that class. In fact, I am rather proud of myself for trying it – and then knowing myself and honoring that. But I'm even happier that I am truly comfortable with who I really am. When it comes to exercise, I am a hiker, and a walker, and a skier, and a kayaker, and a biker, and a snowshoer, and a rollerblader, and a passionate yogi. I am not a kickboxer.

Perhaps the most important choice you will make in the context of exercise is what you like to do. Look for the fun things, the things that sound to you like play. Golf, frisbee, hide-and-seek, dance, hula-hooping, gardening, volleyball, tennis, rollerblading, ping-pong, squash, Tai Chi... Take the time to get to know yourself and really consider what you would love to do - then do it. It's the only way it will last.

Again, as with making adjustments to your relationship with food, start slow and take it easy on yourself. For some people - including my kickboxing friend mentioned above - working up a vigorous sweat at 5am is exactly the kind of thing they love. It feeds them, above and beyond the benefits to their physical well-being. If you, like I, are not that kind of person, find your "thing" and start small.

When I first took up yoga, I went to one class a week & I really enjoyed it. I found myself looking forward to it. Then I found myself fiercely defending that time-slot in my schedule. And eventually I wanted more of it.

A couple years into my personal yoga practice, I was going four to six times a week for at least an hour. As my life changed, and the seasons changed, my schedule changed. I found I had dropped back to only once per week. I felt bad about it, and not because I thought I 'should' be doing it more often, but because I had LOVED it. I loved the way my body felt, I loved what it did for my mental state, I loved the little successes every time I was able to do a pose I hadn't done before… so, I started small again.

Now, half a decade later, I have my own healthy balance. I generally practice yoga 3-5 times per week. Sometimes for an hour, sometimes for 15 minutes. I love the way I feel when I take time to start my day that way, but I don't come down on myself for not doing it often or long enough. I also bike, hike and/or walk with my dog, ski, kayak, swim, rollerblade, or any number of other things every week. That particular combination of yoga-and-something is the best balance for me, right now in my life. That's not to say it won't change. And I still start small; on busy days I only "commit" myself to 15 minutes of yoga. Sometimes I'm in the groove and I love it and I find more time, so I practice for an hour or more… sometimes, I get through my 15 minutes and that's all I've got in me - for whatever reason. But I promised myself I'd get at least 15 minutes of yoga, at least three days per week and that, I know I can do.

Make a Plan

As has been suggested in many, many other texts and by many, many experts, deciding that you are going to suddenly start an exercise and diet plan, and then expecting yourself to wake up an hour early, every morning, for the rest of your life and do the thing you've decided to do, doesn't often work. Approach nurturing yourself as a pleasure you are choosing to make time for, an expression of how much you love yourself. Then commit to making SOME time for it.

Start at a point where you feel truly comfortable; with the change, the activity, the frequency, the duration.

Find a way to feel genuinely excited about the plan. Let the passion and appreciation for it grow within your heart.

You almost certainly will find that you soon love caring for yourself in this way so much that it is a pleasure you don't want to live without.

Love the way you PLAY in your body and in your life.

2

Clean Mental Self

Presence

Life in our modern world is one of action and distraction...
and often absence. Whether by accident or by design, we
largely spend our time DOING one thing while we are
THINKING another. To a degree, some of this is natural. You
will quite likely think about work while you're driving across
town or think about dinner while you are grocery shopping.
Often, however, the truth is we are far more distracted than
that. We're not just *aware* of passing thoughts while we're
working through a day, our mind is not just wandering... it
truly *is* in another place; at our friend's recent birthday party,
at our child's school, running down last night's discussion with
our partner... and it doesn't quit when we go home. In fact,
we likely distract ourselves even further; we turn the TV on
while we cook dinner or do the laundry, we stare at our
phones while we watch TV or eat, we make phone calls while
we walk the dog... In truth, then, we are giving none of these
activities our full attention and that mental ping-pong is
exhausting. Our brains are perpetually jumping from one
thought or action or emotion or situation to the next and back
again. That kind of distraction is also programming us to be
perpetually absent in some measure and unable to truly listen
- with our ears, minds, and bodies - leaving us "tuned out"
and disconnected from our soul-selves.

Worse still, in putting our minds somewhere else – perhaps on the stack of bills that need to be paid – we are drawing that energy; that feeling of lack or fear or anxiety, into the moment we're in, thereby perpetuating the impact of that negative feeling on our overall energy.

Of course, we have to go on living in our fast paced, distracted world. But making time every day for presence can help you tune in to your soul self and harness the power you have there.

Your body and your mind are constantly responding to energy cues. If you can slow down, connect to yourself and your body, you may just "hear" more messages from god - your own god-force energy. Choose presence.

Ordinary Presence

Mindfulness takes focus and to begin, it may be helpful to adopt the previous mantra of 'start small'. Perhaps by choosing a daily task & committing to working through it with a present mind; slowly, without the distraction of music, television, or anything else.

Even something as mundane as folding laundry can be a valuable training opportunity for your brain and can allow the subconscious part of your mind to open you up to some deeper insights.

If you are struggling with this exercise, try slowing down even more. Work through the task as though you are operating in slow motion. To keep your mind from wandering, focus on the task at hand - or even just your hands. For example, if you happen to be folding laundry, focus on how the clothes feel, how your fingers look, what colors you see, how those colors make you feel, and so on. Eating this way is a great way to truly connect to your food and how it makes you feel. Yoga is another wonderful tool in this effort. Focusing on your breath while you move your body through a variety of slow, gentle actions will connect your mind with your body, help create a sense of peace and well being, and give your mental muscles a chance to rest.

Particular Presence

This might be something like traditional meditation, or a practice of mental focus. The idea is simply to set aside some time to clear your mind. If you are a high energy person, perhaps letting the body do an automatic task - liking walking - will help to free your mind. Try slowing it down – WAY down. Take a few breaths from a seated position to clear your mind, then focus on standing up; bending at the waist, placing your hands on your knees, pressing into your knees as you engage your abdomen, straighten your back and your legs. Now and add a step. Yes, literally. One step. Pick up one foot and then put it down in front of the other one. Take. A. Single. Step. Breathe. Step. Breathe. Step.

A person more comfortable with stillness might find working with breath alone is an easy way to get into this practice. Sit still, close your eyes, and feel your whole body respond as you slowly inhale, and then slowly exhale. Commit to five breath cycles. Or, take five minutes to get still, with eyes closed, and check in with each part of your body; feel your feet, feel your legs, feel your knees, and so on.

Again, start small. Often people are so overwhelmed and intimidated by the idea of spending some time with an empty mind that they don't do it at all. Just sitting still with a clear (or clear-ing) mind for a single minute or two - 5 or 10 of the breath cycles mentioned above - can make a world of difference in your ability to connect with yourself… and therefore your ability to manifest. A few minutes of mindfulness every day can help you achieve a deeper sense of calm, which can help you tune-in and feel more deeply - all of which helps to "clean" your tuning fork.

Meditation

Meditation can be many things, but for me it's just 'tuning-in' time; giving some attention to how I feel and how *what I want* feels. It is a time to listen to my body and open my subconscious mind. When I first began a practice of meditation, I got all excited if I made it though 5 or ten minutes of stillness. Now, I like to reserve at least a half hour, and generally I go over a little. I truly love the quiet time, I truly love the change in my attitude toward - and energy for - the coming day, and I truly love the delight of imagination.

That last one is big, for me at least. Imagination is a powerful tool to help us create the kind of vibration - the kind of reality – we want to create. Believing in god force as energy, and believing all things have energy, it almost goes without saying that matching the frequency of the life & self you want will practically guarantee it. In fact, I have a framed quote in my bathroom to that effect; "Everything is energy and that's all there is to it. Match the frequency of the reality you want, and you cannot help but get that reality. This is not philosophy, this is physics." ~Albert Einstein

---

Alas, I've never found any credible documentation that directly attributes this quote to that particular genius, and whomever made a poster out of it spelled philosophy 'philosphy', but I find it helpful anyway. To my mind it does a great job of focusing my belief system; match the frequency of the reality I want. For me, that means imagining it. Imagining how it looks, how it *feels*, to have, do, and be the things I want.

Meditation is different for everybody, but here's how mine looks. I currently spend the first few minutes in gratitude. I give thanks for the wonderful things that are already in my life. I look for and acknowledge the little ways in which my dreams have already come true, pat myself on the back for the magic I've already manifested, and take a moment to feel gratitude for the tremendous gift of LIVING. Then I take a moment to clear my mind, and 'get into' my own heart. For me, that involves trying to FEEL my heart; its wealth of love, and joy, and laughter, and warmth… then, I spend the next few minutes visualizing what I want to create - in my day, in my work, in my life - and FEELING how it feels to have/do/be those things. I let a smile come to my face, I let my heart thump with excitement, I let my mind wander over all the wonderful feelings and images until I feel as though I've filled my heart with all those things. I invite god-force energy to help me connect, understand, and change whatever I feel necessary to change in myself in order to create the life I want, and then I settle into quiet.

I don't necessarily believe in a certain form of meditation. But when I heard meditation described as "listening to the Universe", it really rang true for me. That, then, is how I spend the last portion of my meditation time. Listening. Not judging, or wishing, or thinking, or dreaming, or watching… just listening and feeling. Hearing the natural music made by the sound of birds mixed with traffic, the sound of garbage trucks mixed with barking dogs, acknowledging the comfortable feeling of a gentle breeze coming in the window and subtly moving across my skin, the sensations created in my body. When my mind wanders, I tell it to come back to this moment and just listen. Experience. Drink it in.

When I'm done, I give gratitude again, for the time and love I gave myself, and head for my closet to get dressed for the day.

Active Presence

Time Outside

Spending time outdoors is a wonderful way to clean the spiritual "tuning fork". Fresh air is good for the body and soul in ways we've only begun to discover, exercise helps to eliminate toxins from our bodies physically and mentally, and the gentle harmony that exists in the natural world sets a pace that allows for deep connection and introspection. Get outside as often as you can, anywhere you can, for as long as you can. Again, start small. Perhaps walk around the block once a week or sit in the park for 10 minutes on Sunday mornings, and work up from there. Don't worry about whether or not there is traffic nearby (though making an effort to have time out of town in natural silence is valuable). Your body and unconscious mind are picking up all kinds of cues from the natural world; birds and animals, air movement and moisture, temperature and pressure changes... and all of these things encourage your mind to a calmer and more harmonious state.

No matter what you're doing, time outside is a great opportunity to find lots more to be grateful for; sunshine, birds, silence, wind, trees, animals, leaves, color, smells, sounds... all the gifts of life.

Time Alone

Another of our favorite distractions as human beings is each other. Spending time alone, though, is essential to "tuning in" to *your* soul self. Growing closer to someone in any relationship means spending quality time together so it makes sense that the best way to get in touch with yourself is to spend time alone. I don't mean watching TV or browsing the web. ACTIVELY alone is the goal; do something you would do with a romantic interest or best friend; make dinner for yourself - without TV and WITH candle light. Do it slowly, with intention. Go for a walk, play an instrument, read a favorite poem, take a bath, visit an art gallery or museum (just take the self-guided tour). Find a little time regularly to go on a date - with yourself. Make it a priority. Pets are great for this. I've come to some of my most profound understandings of myself, my connection to god force, my role in my little corner of the Universe... on a hiking trail with my dog.

Be present in your time alone. Focus on you. Stop and re-direct thoughts and concern for others. This time is about you. When your mind wanders to others' lives, bring it back to you. Focus on what YOU want, who you are, what you believe, how YOU feel, the incredible life YOU are creating for YOURSELF - and not on what you want another person to do, or be, or give to or for you.

Obviously, many of these premises work well together; for instance, a quiet walk can be a time of active meditation, a gift of love from you to your body in the form of exercise, and a bit of precious alone time. The ultimate goal is still the same; get in touch with your soul-self, your god-self.

Focus on Yourself

This point is so huge and important I found I'd mentioned it over and over and over again – like, WAY too many times - in early drafts of this manuscript.

Why is it such a big deal? There are so many reasons, but here are a few:

1) You will only ever really have control over yourself. So why expend mental energy worrying about the lives of others? Have compassion, listen when your friends or family need to talk, treat everyone with respect, but don't spend time thinking about what others could or should be doing with their lives.

2) It isn't your life, so it isn't your business. Period. You may think you know literally everything about a person – and therefore what is right or wrong in their lives, what they should or shouldn't do - but the truth is there could be all kinds of things happening in the minds and hearts of those we love that they aren't sharing. There may be things happening in their lives that they themselves aren't even aware of. And those little variances could change everything about what is or isn't good for them. It may appear their

decisions are made from a very transparent place, but we never really know.

3) *We never really know.* The path of our lives is entirely unknown to any of us. Perhaps your belief that Sue down the street is raising a bratty child is the very set of circumstances that will make Sue's child the next Mother Theresa. Maybe the guy who doesn't mow his lawn the way you think he should, is harboring a perfect little ecosystem that will someday make his property the last great butterfly sanctuary. Perhaps the person you think is dragging down the whole office environment will be the very person that inspires a co-worker to start the next great tech company. There is no way to know how another person's life will be impacted by the decisions they make, so leave them to their own.

4) It can often come across as critical or judgmental – perhaps because it is. Think you can "get around it" by just keeping your judgments to yourself? Not so. Even if you don't tell others about it, you are programming your computer to judge, and eventually you will likely find it judging you.

(The reverse is also true: programming your mind to think positive, loving thoughts about people regardless of your impression of them and their lives, also programs your mind to think those same kinds of things about you.)

5) No one can ever perfectly meet the emotional needs of another person. Ever. Because you will never be able to love anyone as perfectly as they can love themselves – if they get the chance and choose to take it. Your love for YOURSELF is what matters. And others' love for THEMSELVES.

Ultimately, concerning yourself with the lives of others is a waste of your energy. If you want to change your relationship with others, put the effort into changing yourself. If you want a romantic partner, focus on loving yourself, on the love you feel, the *kind of person* you want to share your life with… not what you want one particular person to do or be. If you want a more peaceful relationship with your kids, focus on the love you have for them, the wonderful parts of the relationship as it is, your love for yourself as a parent.

Whatever you want from or with others… create it first in yourself. Clear your mind of any worry for the lives of others. They got it.

I have lots of beautiful-soul friends, and two of them in particular are more like beautiful-soul-sisters. They've been roommates off and on for years, they've been friends since they were little girls and they've been driving each other crazy since day one.

They're a classic odd couple; one is a little OCD and a fastidious housekeeper. The other is an artist and flits from one project to another, leaving a wake of clothes, jewelry, paint, beads, coffee cups and dishes throughout the house. After one particularly rough window of time, my friend (we'll call her Pam) and I had coffee, and she told me she felt on the brink of explosion. She made breakfast, packed a lunch, and prepared dinner for her roommate (we'll call her Denise). Pam cleaned the house for Denise, looked for jobs when Denise complained about the one she had, organized Denise's art space… but Denise did not seem grateful, and didn't even seem to want to spend as much time together. Denise almost never took out the trash, or said she loved her lunch, or brought Pam a present…

When I had lunch with Denise the next afternoon (yes, literally, the next day. It's a long story.) she mentioned how hard she'd been trying to remember to start the dishwasher or feed the dog the way Pam wanted. She was grateful for lunch and dinner, but afraid to tell Pam that she'd actually planned on eating something else. She'd stopped watching movies with Pam at night because she liked to make jewelry while she did so, and it drove Pam crazy when she dropped beads. In general, she felt like she had was living on pins and needles.

Through the course of the first conversation Pam realized she had been taking care of Denise because she felt like she had to. She felt like Denise couldn't take care of herself. But Denise had never asked for her to help in those ways. She also realized how much pressure she'd been putting on their friendship, pressure on Denise to be happy and grateful in the right way... to love her back in the right way... without even realizing it.

Pam knew Denise loved her and cherished their friendship. And she realized she'd always known Denise would never be the kind of person who cleaned the house the way Pam did.

The 'ah-ha!' moment came when Pam realized that Denise would only ever be able to take care of herself if she was given the opportunity to do so. Pam accepted that if she wanted a clean house, she would have to do it, AND do it because it was something she wanted to do – for *herself*. She'd also have to do it without shaming Denise for not doing so. Denise came to a similar conclusion; she knew that Pam was only showing her love and realized that if she were more honest and up front with Pam about what she wanted and needed, it would ultimately help them both.

Pam realized she had to accept that Denise would show her love in other ways; by making her art or buying her favorite coffee – and that if Pam could love herself enough, *whatever* Denise did to show her love and friendship, would be enough.

Weeks later, Pam called to tell me she'd stopped making meals for Denise, she'd stopped looking for jobs for her, and tidying up her spaces. And they were getting along better than ever. Pam was also excited about her new-found time and energy to put into the things she'd been wanting to do for herself; taking a class, gardening, and camping.

Good news! But how did it get so messy in the first place? I think it's because somewhere along the line we began equating loving someone with taking care of them – like parents do. But outside the parent-child relationship that situation isn't particularly healthy. It isn't even healthy in parent-child relationships past the early years.

Making someone else's physical or emotional needs – or both – more important than our own is inherently flawed for oh-so-many reasons.

1) It suggests the other person isn't capable of taking care of themselves, or isn't doing it "right", and it robs them of the opportunity to take responsibility for, and power over, their own lives.

2) It sets everyone up for failure because you will never be able to truly take care of someone else's emotional or physical needs, exactly the way they would want.

3) It sends the message to your subconscious mind that you aren't worth as much as the other person because you are taking care of them instead of yourself.

4) It puts an implied pressure on them to be grateful, or reciprocate, or at least be happy… so happy and grateful that in their expression of gratitude they can somehow fill us

up with happy too.... all of which is way too much to ask of any relationship.

   5) It leaves no time or energy to put into your own life. Even if the person receiving your 'service' and care *could* give you 'all the gratitude,' it would never fill you up the way truly, deeply loving your own god-self would. So now you are left walking around a little empty all the time – and still needing to take care of your own emotional needs.

"But we're supposed to help each other!" I know. I hear you. And I agree! Plus, it feels WONDERFUL to help someone! I love to help people... if they WANT the help.

   I used to catch myself trying to 'help' people who never actually asked me for help. It happened a lot. And, invariably, no matter how delicately I delivered my unsolicited advice or service, it almost always came off as judgment or criticism or charity and I could feel my friend or family member energetically pull away or shut down. (And when it happened to me, *I* pulled away too.)

   Eventually I realized that more often than not, friends were coming to me not for answers, but because they needed to be *heard*. Often the sheer act of listening helped them feel better, and, occasionally, as they spoke about the situation, THEY realized what they learned, or what they really wanted, or how to handle it going forward. Which is a WAY better situation. Admittedly, reigning in the desire to help, to get involved and 'make it better', is an exercise in restraint. Especially when we're SURE we have the answer. I'm still working on it. But I'm getting better at it and it's getting easier.

   When it comes to the lives of others, we must shut our mouths and trust the soul.

We can never really, truly understand another person's situation so we can never really have the 'right' answers anyway. And even if they do what we want them to do, it wasn't really their decision – it was ours – and so it is inherently less powerful. Plus, there could be all kinds of other lessons that person may have learned should they have had the chance to experience their reality the way they had created it; without our input.

When you find yourself wanting to "help" (change) someone, especially if they haven't asked for it, instead consider using the situation as an opportunity to see yourself more clearly.

When I find myself mentally working through a conversation with someone about their lives and catch myself wanting to "change" them or their perspective, I try to stop and see what I'm really after. Often, I want to be 'right'. That's a sure sign for me to shut up. They don't need to validate my belief system or perspective. I am only 'right' for me, and they can be 'right' too, even if our perspectives are different. Other times, I feel disrespected or bullied and what I'm really looking for is a chance to make them see their error. Again, a sure sign that I need to look at it differently. It's not my job to change the way they see themselves or what they believe. It *is* a chance for me to re-define my boundaries in the relationship, and re-asses what I want out of the relationship.

Yes, there have been cases in my life – and there will be again - wherein someone's unsolicited advice was quite valuable and presented me with an idea I never would have considered. Why are these situations different?

Because they are authentic. And usually accidental. And almost always just ideas tossed in my general direction – not dictatorial instructions. In these cases, it usually feels as though I landed in a brainstorming session I wasn't planning on and it feels like excited, supportive, idea-sharing... so I can see it that way and accept it joyfully. I use the same metric to decide if that's what someone is asking of me. If so, I let my ideas for their projects or their lives come pouring out of me. Otherwise, I silently wish them well, bless them with love and light, and bite my tongue.

I strive to really listen to people, determine if they want my help or they want my compassion and – in both cases - I focus on building them up. If they have asked for my advice, I give it, and encourage them toward what I hear them saying *they* want or believe. That way, I figure I'm covered: it supports them in becoming who they truly are, walking their own path, and connecting to their own soul-self... AND speaking the words aloud and projecting that kind of respect, appreciation, and love will only create more of it to be reflected around the world.

The key here is authenticity. I can smell a "positive-reinforcement-agenda" a mile away. I'm sure you can too.

Don't give instructions (or worse, "encouragement treats") to get me to do / be / live the way you think I should. We can all feel it when we're being manipulated, particularly if we're well connected to our soul-selves. And as uncomfortable as this truth may be, anytime we try to alter a person's behavior, belief system, personality trait or anything else, we ARE manipulating them. If they are actually asking for help, though, or seeking out a way to change themselves or their lives, it's just offering ideas. I know, I know. Confusing. Fuzzy grey line stuff.

As you tune in to yourself, you'll be able to feel it. Really. I promise. And until then, try using this test: if you have an agenda, hold your tongue. If there's a little voice whispering something like "tell them this and maybe they'll do that," shut your mouth, and instead send them light and love and then step back and watch them manifest the life *they* want, the life *their* soul-self, *their* god-self wants, and focus on your own.

Love your relationships – by loving others enough to trust them to their path.

Take Pride

I don't know how it became such a naughty word. Pride. Maybe I do know. As a kid, pride meant, well, pride. Superiority. Self-righteousness. It meant thinking of oneself as higher than. Pride was a sin. Period. As an adult, however, when I reflect on the meaning of the word, there are several layers. Yes, boastful arrogance is one of them. But it's only one. There are several other meanings related to treating something as a treasure, self esteem in general, and - happily for me and my message here - taking pleasure in accomplishment. Perhaps pride is a terribly overlooked gift of the human condition.

I *want* to do things I'm proud of doing. I *want* to be proud of the way I treated someone, the way I treat myself. I *want* to be proud of the work I do or the personal-best record I broke. I think pride becomes 'bad' when it is used to make ourselves *better or more important than another person*. So, don't compare. Take pride in YOU. It's a great tool - particularly in helping you love yourself. Every time your mind wanders to something in the I'm-not-good-enough category, stop it and redirect it to something which gives you a sense of pride. Perhaps you passed on the second cookie at coffee yesterday, or maybe you spent 3 extra minutes in meditation, or maybe you successfully manifested a trip out of town next month. Whatever it is, find your pride and run with it. Use it to remind yourself over and over that you are magnificent, special, beautiful, talented, important, valuable, and above all else - LOVED. By yourself, at the very least. Because look at those wonderful things you did / thought / achieved!! You did it! You embodied your best self! Well done!

Love the way you take pride in, and love, your god-self.

3

Clean Spiritual Self

Love Yourself

If making self-love your first priority sounds selfish, you're not alone. It did for me too. But when I really considered the perspective of a life lived in service to others *above and over* service to myself, I could see the flaws in the plan. (See: Focus on Yourself). And I understood what my teachers had been trying to tell me.

Imagine if we were all taking care of each other's emotional health, managing each other's feelings or lives. That scenario leaves us all waiting around for someone else to make us feel loved, fulfilled, happy, successful… and, we have to settle for whatever version of that they can give. If waiting for 10 minutes in traffic makes you crazy, imagine waiting for *years* for someone to fully, deeply, understand you and know how to make you happy. There's a good chance you'll wait your whole life. There's also a chance it will never happen. (In my opinion that last one is a guarantee – nobody will ever *make* you feel fully loved, fulfilled, happy, successful or whatever. Because nobody will ever really know you and what you want to feel the way you know yourself.)

Loving yourself; your body, your personality, your mind, your reality, your whole *life*, first and foremost… celebrating it deeply and honestly from the heart… that is the greatest way to show gratitude and appreciation for the gift of life you were given.

Focusing on most perfectly loving our god-selves makes us responsible for our own happiness, connects us to our god-force energy, and absolves us of any need to get involved in the emotional well-being of others, (our PERCEPTION of THEIR emotional well-being. You see the problem). Which in turn serves to empower them to take control and responsibility over their own lives. Arguably a better situation all the way around.

Even the messages of my childhood church seem to carry an under-appreciated message of self love – at least in my mind. If I am made in God's image, doesn't it make sense that my top priority would be to love myself completely – the reflection of Him in me - the way He loves me? And in so doing, loving both the gift of life I've been given, and "Him" (whomever you believe Him to be) more completely.

Prioritizing your expressions of love to yourself; your self-protection, your respect for yourself… isn't selfish. It is truly loving God, the temple you are, and the life you've been given. It's also, in part, a service to others.

The way we love ourselves is as individual and varied as we are; for some, loving yourself as perfectly as possible may mean living a life of service to others – because it FEEDS you, because you love *yourself* in those roles. Not because you "should" do them, but because you genuinely feel it is a way you show deep, true, love - for *yourself* - and therefore god, and all god elements. Choosing to serve others because you "should" or because it's the "right thing to do" or because you want to be seen as charitable or giving can lead to resentment on your part and guilt or shame on the part of the receiver. But choosing to serve others because you

WANT to, because you LOVE to, feeds you and everyone else involved. Performed as expressions of self-love, acts of service build up the provider as well as the recipient and make it possible to give and receive even more.

For others, our deepest showing and action of god-self love, of self love in general, is just that: truly and fundamentally loving ourselves. The repercussions of that self love ripple out and become evident in every facet of our lives; the way we parent, or the way we work, or the way we treat our friends and strangers… the way we live our lives in general *as a result of the way we love ourselves*. In this way, for many, loving ourselves is – in and of itself – an act of service.

When I began to truly live self-love in my heart and in my day-to-day choices, I was happier, and brought that happiness into the lives of others. I was more at peace and more comfortable with myself, and that helped those around me find comfort in themselves. I was more successful in my career, so I was able to show love through donations of money and mindful shopping; supporting local artists, producers of anything and everything, and service providers. I had more energy, a better attitude, and was able to shary time, my knowledge (when requested), and my genuine love for people and their professional endeavors more freely.

Loving my life; feeling full-to-bursting with gratitude for myself, for my experiences, for my gifts and challenges, *is* – for me - loving god, and all those around me.

Perhaps, if we can see each other - ALL people - as elements of god, then loving *ourselves* becomes both a contribution to a greater god force, and an expression of love to others in our ability to share with them our lightest, purest, highest god-self. Seeing others as elements of god also – hopefully -

cultivates greater respect and appreciation for ALL the forms of god in our worlds.

You deserve to love yourself. You're great! Everyone else is too. Your greatness does not detract from the greatness of another, and theirs does not detract from you. Your goal is to love who you are *without* any kind of "measuring stick". You love yourself simply because you are exactly *who you WANT to be.*

Of course, this is both a HUGE concept and one within which countless great minds have pondered and taught. I do not intend to challenge or endorse any particular idea - I am simply offering my experience; learning to love myself was and is a *constant, life-long practice…* and the rewards are beyond description.

In my early adult years, I was finally able to grasp the importance of self love, albeit in a very cerebral way. I "got" the *why*, but I had no idea where to begin with the *how.* For me, this was the real truth at the center of the years I spent trying to "find myself"; it wasn't just about understanding who I was and who I wanted to be - although that was a big part of the process too. It was about finding a version of myself I was proud to be – a version of myself I could LOVE. When I finally realized I could create myself as whomever I wanted to be simply by choosing things that aligned with that vision, I began to understand why I hadn't been able to love myself before. I had been trying to love who I was *in the eyes of others*, the roles I was playing in their lives. I loved being loved as the perfect girlfriend, I loved being loved as the perfect daughter, I loved being loved as the perfect employee... but I was just acting out a role I thought those people wanted me to play.

Which led me to realize I was a woman who loved *to the exclusion of self*. I didn't know who I was and so I just became whomever I thought those I loved wanted me to be. A perfect daughter, living within the guidelines of my parent's wishes (at least as far as they knew). A perfect girlfriend, interested in whatever he was interested in (at least as far as he knew), and at his side almost entirely for *his* benefit. A perfect friend, the one who called enough, remembered every birthday, knew when to send flowers or chocolate. A perfect sister, the one who had all the answers. A perfect employee. A perfect neighbor. And on and on ad infinitum. I hadn't been choosing who *I* wanted to be, and I hadn't been loving the real me. I *thought* I was showing others love by attempting to morph into whatever kind of person I thought they wanted. And then waiting for them to love me. So I could love me. Which, of course, was – and is - impossible. And a little crazy.

Ultimately, it was both exhausting and fruitless. As we all know, we can never be perfect, and we can certainly never know how to be someone else's perfect anything. Not to mention that attempting to be perfect robbed those I loved of getting the "real" me - so of course it felt forced and somewhat insincere. A mess. A failure. And it was the only way I knew to show love to others. Worse still I had no idea how to love myself because I had no idea who I really was or who I really wanted to be.

Years of introspection and practice finally got me to the point where I began to understand who I truly was and how I showed love to others - which gave me great clues in learning how to love myself. I also finally understood how incredibly good, and honest, and fulfilling it is to be loved for who you REALLY are - not the 'perfect' version, but the beautifully flawed version. And, it felt great to love others authentically. Imperfectly, yes. But honestly. Deeply.

It was invigorating instead of exhausting and freed me from trying to behave in a way that would "earn" the love I wanted – which often looked like throwing darts at the board anyway; 'Is *this* what you (boyfriend, friend, boss, parent, sibling) want me to do / be?'. It also took the pressure off my relationships; I was no longer disappointed in the way other people loved me. I was no longer longing for them to love me differently, more, or "enough". Now I could just enjoy the love I got from them, however they chose to show it, and it was always enough because I was already fulfilled.

I think I was nearly 30 years old before I understood what self-love really meant, and it took the guidance of many wise souls to help me learn to truly *live* self-love. To feel the love I had nurtured for myself deep in my heart. To love myself in *action*, not just in concept. To love myself in stillness & solitude. To love myself in faults, moments of weakness, 'bad' decisions and the like is still a constant effort.

Loving myself more deeply is truly the primary focus of my spiritual growth. Loving myself blatantly… my big, huge, beautiful soul self - right out there in the open for everyone to see. My loud self. My clumsy self. My distracted self. My brazen self. My passionate self. My insecure self. My wise self. My silly self. My naive self. Loving my weird, crazy, uniquely beautiful self takes effort, but it's getting easier. Not that I don't want to continue to work on my issues… of course I do. But I also want to love myself anyway. Completely. WITH those flaws. I want to stop holding myself to some unattainable standard of perfect and love myself completely, exactly as I am, because I finally have a deep appreciation for who I really am and the gift that is my life. I know what kind of person I want to be and what kind of life I want to live so I can choose which person, or response, or situation, or work, or opportunity or whatever, that fits with that self. And that has been one of the greatest blessings of really knowing and loving myself: I can use that understanding as a compass for my life and trust my decisions.

I can't tell you how to love yourself; it's different for everybody. But I can tell you what helped me.

Make a List

One of my many wonderful, wise teachers suggested that if I felt like I didn't know how to love myself I could begin by simply doing the things for myself that I would do for anyone else I loved; feeding myself good food, saving money or time to take myself on a weekend getaway or get a massage, praising myself for the good I had done or the successes I'd had, reminding myself that I was valuable and skilled. It sounds so incredibly simple - and in truth it is - but it was a huge idea for me. So, I embarked on a personal mission to get to know myself and find out what I loved. Then give or do those things to and for myself. I started by making lists… in notebooks and on sticky notes all over the house. Lists about what kind of clothes, music, and food I liked, what kind of place I wanted to live, what my priorities were in terms of happiness, what success looked like to me… ALL. KINDS. OF. LISTS. Guests may have thought me crazy – but I didn't care. It helped me. And who knows, maybe when they saw my note on the bathroom mirror to 'see joy', it helped them to love themselves and their lives more, too.

I made lists about what I wanted in a relationship, lists about what I wanted in my professional life, lists about what I wanted to keep in my refrigerator. (Seriously, you can learn something about a person based on what they like to eat - and what they DECIDE to eat.) The most important one, though, was the list about the *kind* of person I was - otherwise known as the Alphabet List.

Because I had no idea who I really was at this point, I felt truly and utterly worthless. I couldn't find a single thing I liked - much less loved - about myself, and the prospect of telling myself about my own good qualities was more than daunting... it was flat-out inconceivable. So, one of my wise mentors suggested I start doing the Alphabet List. "What I like about myself: A... I'm amicable. B... I can be brave, sometimes. C... I'm curious," and so on. It was hard, at first, and it seemed ridiculous to say the least. But the truth is, it helped. I started to see myself as valuable and worth loving – worth my own love. It was a massive shift that changed everything in my life for the better – and it happened quickly.

After several months I rather quit doing the alphabet list, because I had a real appreciation for who I was and the wonderful qualities that made me, me. And that gave me something to love.

I still do this exercise when I'm feeling low. Though I don't necessarily adhere to the alphabet, I do take a moment to remind myself about the reasons I love being me. That appreciation and gratitude help me remember that I deserve the wonderful things I've manifested in my life. I deserve the wonderful things that I will manifest today and tomorrow and next year... and so do you. But you must DEEPLY believe that. You must know, at the very core of your being, that you deserve the things you want to manifest in your life, and you must love yourself enough to *give them to yourself.*

Respect Yourself

I imagine it would be hard to truly, deeply love someone you don't respect. So – respect yourself. Teach others how valuable you are by valuing (respecting) yourself.

There are lots of ways to do that, of course. The first and easiest way - in my opinion - starts with being proud of the decisions you've made and the person you are.

I remember wishing as a newly minted adult, that I were the kind of person confident enough to wear a hat. Or a pair of plaid pants. Or a funky shirt. But I was so afraid of what others would think I stuck to jeans and t-shirts. When I really found the love and respect for myself, I totally got over it and found the freedom to wear whatever I wanted. I know there are people who look at me funny. I genuinely don't care. And if someone comments on my hat or my funky pants or my pile of faux pearls draped playfully around my neck, I own it. With humor as often as I can. I take it as a compliment – whether they meant it that way or not. Because I happen to like my unique-ness, and I LOVE that I am finally the kind of person who knows what I like and isn't afraid to be different. I am proud of myself and my choices.

Another way you respect yourself is by teaching others how you want to be treated. And you do that by treating them exactly that way. Don't demand respect. Command it. By first treating others – all others – with respect. Even those who disrespect you.

And respect yourself enough to accept and acknowledge when you're wrong. We're all wrong sometimes. Our mistakes can help us grow if we can love ourselves enough to admit that we were wrong – to ourselves and anyone we may have hurt – and see ways we want to change ourselves. Personally, I find it infinitely more empowering to step up and admit mistakes than hiding from their truth. And, I find others respond with much more compassion and understanding when I've wronged them. Erring is human and perhaps we can more easily forgive, and even connect with each other, when we can admit we aren't perfect.

Sometimes that means acknowledging that we were not intentionally mis-treated. Many times I've caught myself feeling defensive when the other person had no intention of disrespecting me. Take a moment to determine whether you are truly the victim of disrespect, or if you might be defensive because of your own emotional history. Maybe you feel disrespected and judged because you are judging yourself. If that's the case, you can choose to change your response.

If you were genuinely treated with disrespect, you get to choose your response to that too. Perhaps start by holding some compassion and accepting the possibility that those treating you badly with criticism or judgment are doing so because they are harshly judging themselves. Then, let it go.

Here's where loving yourself really pays off. If you can love and respect yourself enough, the judgement or criticism (disrespect) of another means nothing. You can choose to love yourself so completely, so deeply, that the opinion of another does not negatively impact you – because you don't need their love and validation to feel whole or wonderful or important. Love yourself so much that if someone makes a disparaging comment – about your glasses, for instance - you can respond by telling them how much you love your new spectacles. Or if they suggest you are fat, you can tell them how much you love your curves & your body. Or if they imply you are unintelligent, you can laugh at yourself for whatever "stupid" thing you may have said or done and walk away - knowing you are smart, that their opinion was based on a singular moment unrepresentative of your whole self, and that it doesn't matter anyway.

Please Note: Respecting yourself, standing up for yourself, does NOT mean turning the disrespect you've been shown back around on offender. In the previous examples you will note that I suggest owning your own power, taking pride in who you are, and showing your love for yourself… NOT "tattling", name-calling, or temper-tantrum-throwing. These responses only give the person disrespecting you – the bully, if you will – exactly what they want; power over you. And additional justifications for their actions.

Stand in your power, in your love and respect for yourself. Be the bigger, more empowered, more loving person. Have compassion, treat the "offender" with respect, and then love yourself enough to address it or walk away. Because not only is their opinion irrelevant to your life, you are more important to yourself than any role they play. You deserve to be respected for who you are, what you believe, and the choices you make – as long as they are not harming others.

If, however, you find yourself in a relationship where you are truly being repeatedly disrespected, love yourself enough to do something about it. Love yourself enough to discuss it or just move on.

I, personally, am a big fan of second chances and often when I have defined my boundaries of respect by walking away (verbally, virtually, or otherwise) from someone, the message is clearly received. Should they seek me out again and this time, treat me with respect, I am delighted to forgive, forget, and jump right back in to the relationship as if nothing happened.

However, allowing yourself to be disrespected over and over is never appropriate. That can quickly become abuse and abuse is never ok. Address it, and if genuine abuse continues, seek the support or advice of someone you trust. Find a way to stand in your power – even if that means leaving the relationship altogether.

There are, at least for me, a couple rare exceptions. As human beings in relationships and families and work environments, expecting people to treat us with respect OR simply walking out of their lives are not always the only options.

There are a couple cases in my life where I could be (and for a long time, I was) hurt by the judgments, statements, or criticisms of people close to me. They really were judgments, and they really were from people I loved. However, because they are who they are, I choose to continue to participate in relationships with them, knowing they will continue to disrespect me. I do this because I have discussed my feelings with these particular people on several occasions and I understand that in their minds, they are not disrespecting me, they're helping. They truly believe they know better than I what is right in my life.

In these special cases, I have chosen to simply acknowledge that the relationship is more important to me than one I can walk away from. And that these people are simply in a completely different place than I. It is not my job to judge his or her path, his or her choices, his or her 'right' or 'wrong'-ness… So, when I feel disrespected, in these cases, I acknowledge the feeling to myself, take a moment to remember that this is not actually about me, and hold compassion for the person across from me. And (this is the really important part), I CHOOSE *not to be hurt* because I know he or she doesn't mean to hurt me. I remind myself that I love who I am, and that is what matters to me. Then I respond with something polite, like "I understand your perspective," change the subject and move on.

I am not saying this is the ideal way to handle relationships. I'm saying there are a variety of ways to keep your relationships, HOLD respect for ALL others, and still command respect for yourself. Get to your center – your real god-self core – and find the method that works for you. The one that makes you LOVE the way you treat others and LOVE the way you respect yourself. The one that makes you LOVE the way you think about others and think about yourself.

And for those relationships that just aren't working for you, particularly romantic ones…

Let Go

Love yourself so powerfully that you have no need for any other person or situation to validate, care for, or love you. Expecting or even hoping another person can "make" you feel a certain way sets everyone up for failure. They, because they will never fully be able to meet your expectations and you, because they will always disappoint you. Now they will likely feel like a failure, which only intimidates them in future attempts. In addition, focusing on how they need to act to make you feel a certain thing demands so much of their time and energy they have none to give themselves; limited resources to make themselves happy. So now that's your job – and no matter how good you think you are, you'll fail at it too. It's a perfect storm for codependency - and utter exhaustion. Imagine living your life perpetually worried about how you are or aren't making someone else happy! (By the way, if you are doing this, don't feel bad about it. Lots of people do. I was one of them. I still am sometimes. I'm working on it.)

Instead, choose to change the dynamic. Let go of the idea that you "need" this particular person in your life. Love yourself so much that you are just fine "alone", or free of the relationship. Maybe even more than "fine". Maybe even *gasp* *happy!* Not only does this free you to let go of any person or situation that isn't working for you, it also makes you *more* attractive, at least in my opinion.

Someone who loves themselves deeply – not in the narcissistic, superficial way, but as a soul-god being on this planet – is infinitely more attractive.

Your ability to meet your own needs in terms of feeling loved, validated, pretty, smart, successful, whatever... means you don't come off as needy. You don't need anyone to do any of that for you because you already know and love yourself. That makes it so much easier for them to love you, however they can and want to. AND – it's just icing on your cake because you already feel loved, validated, pretty, smart, successful or whatever.

In relationships it also means they don't need to worry about always trying to "make" you happy, so they can relax and focus on making themselves happy – which means you don't have to make them happy! You can just love them when and how *you* want to and enjoy their happy energy in your life.

They can live their own lives and you can live yours, each beautifully complimenting and celebrating the other. There's no pressure to "complete" you, to be your everything, to ponder endlessly on how to make YOU happy. You both get to just BE happy. Individually. Together.

While letting go of "needing" others is essential, in my mind, remember that SHOWING love to others – without *expectation* of their emotion, or response, or reciprocation – is a beautiful way to nurture a relationship. Show love. DO. PLEASE do. Show love the way you want to – without expectation. Because you want to, because that's what you do for things and people in your life that you deem precious. Not because you feel you need to take care of another person's feelings.

If you aren't feeling loved, before you blame your partner (or parent or sibling or whatever) try to see how they ARE showing you love. Maybe in a gentle touch, or a strong work ethic, or a sparkling clean house. Perhaps they're just showing love in ways you didn't expect to see. Then love YOURSELF. If it still isn't enough, it might be time to let go.

This is also true in professional relationships. Not needing a title (or to be the boss's favorite, or whatever) to feel valuable or validated means you can have authentic relationships with all those around you. You can work for the reasons you love your work (yes, you might have to look really hard to find those sometimes. We'll touch on that later.) And you can free yourself to leave if the job isn't working for you.

In almost every relationship context, focusing on and taking care of your own needs, emotionally and otherwise, will make you both a better and perhaps a more attractive version of yourself to share with whomever you choose, however you choose.

Teach people how to treat you – how to SEE you – in the way you treat yourself and others. Focus on and love yourself, and you'll set yourself – and the other beautiful souls in your life – free.

Accept Your Power

One of my wise mentors called us "co-creators" of our lives, our realities. That term fits for many people so I will use it here.

I understand what she's getting at, but I get a little hung up on the "co" portion of the word. I think it could be construed to refer to only a tiny portion of our lives when personally, I believe quite the opposite. I believe we create the *vast majority* of our reality. Owning the truth that you are the MAJORITY creator of your life, your reality, is incredibly empowering. It can also be somewhat daunting. But let's start by focusing on the good stuff; the empowerment.

In my first book, *The Me I Was,* I mention this same concept and use the following example; If you go out for a walk, and you focus on the feeling of the sun on your skin, the sound of the birds singing, the beautiful image of leaves dancing on the trees... that sense of wonder and magic, that beautiful experience will be your reality. If, however, you were to go on the same walk and instead focus on the child screaming, the rain clouds on the horizon, the trash blowing around and the smell of dog poo, THAT will be your reality. You choose your experience. Your belief about yourself and your reality creates it around you. You ALWAYS have a choice. Choose to see the good and celebrate it. Thank yourself for creating it.

Instead of being intimidated by the responsibility of creating your own reality, see the good; the excitement, the power. Focus on the good in yourself, in your life, in the reality you are in and in the reality you want to create. The reality YOU have created. Acknowledge that anything you lack is either just a mis-perception (meaning you don't truly lack it, you just don't see or recognize it), or an energetic block within you where YOU are withholding that which your soul-self desires, that which it deserves. Maybe because on some level you don't believe you deserve it or your soul doesn't actually want or need it. Maybe you just can't imagine yourself – really see or feel yourself - with it. The point is, if 'something' is standing in the way of the reality you want, accept the truth that the something is you. And empower yourself to change.

Once you accept the power that comes with creating your own reality, you allow yourself - and your incredibly powerful mind - to open the door of perception, and resonate with the energy of what you want, bringing it directly, powerfully, and tangibly into your life.

Love the life you've created. Even the 'bad' things. They are just opportunities so love them too. But especially love the good, love your power to create, love your life.

Take Ownership

While, in my opinion, each of these elements is absolutely essential in mastering manifestation, this one is big. And a little abstract, so stay with me here.

Giving 'ownership' of your life to anyone or anything - particularly circumstances - other than yourself completely eliminates any power you have over your own life. While circumstances do impact us, they are not our definitions. We have the opportunity to choose to see them as something else - and when we do, they will be.

This is another prime place for gratitude. I'm grateful for the motorcycle accident that literally took my life - albeit for only a few moments - and changed it forever. I love who I am now, and that experience profoundly impacted my life and shaped me as a person. While the looks I get when I say it scream 'Are you crazy?!' the truth is that I am deeply grateful for that experience. Incredibly grateful. And I truly believe my soul-self asked for it.

The 'victim mentality' (Poor me! This-or-that happened to me!) is not only socially uncomfortable for many (for me, it's down right annoying), it also completely demeans your power, your gift of choice, and your god-ness. It makes what happens to you everyone else's fault or responsibility. For a life of manifestation to be possible, you must choose to accept full and complete responsibility for your life. Not just your "reaction to it". While of course you can't control others (why would you anyway? That just takes away THEIR power), and you really do only have control over how you REACT to others, you CAN accept that you are drawing certain people & relationships into your life for a reason. The same thing with situations; while you can't control how your boss treats you at work, you CAN accept that you have control over whether or not you work there, whether or not your annoying boss has something to teach you (on a soul level or a professional one), whether or not you choose to find your job tedious or valuably challenging, and so on.

Take ownership for EVERYTHING in your life. Accept that - on some level - you are creating these experiences, these relationships, these situations because your god-self wants them.

If you don't like the experience / relationship / situation, look for the lesson your soul-self may be trying to learn. Look for the ways you can change. Or, take control and change your situation. (Just be aware that if there is a lesson you need to learn, and you change your situation without growing yourself, the lesson will likely come right back to you in another context, person, or situation.) Tune into yourself to see what lessons your soul self may be teaching you in your historical patterns and current situations. Then use your tools (I'll give you some ideas later) to put effort toward growth and change in yourself, and you'll manifest the change you want in your life.

Love the experiences and opportunities you are creating.

Look for the Lesson and Do the Work

You; the embodiment of the universal god-force energy that you are, your soul-self, is always sending you messages about what you need and want. Look around. What isn't working in your life? What messages can you find in those situations? What work can you do?

Decades ago when I was newly single, broke, and back in my hometown, I found myself yearning for what I had just left; my old life – not the old relationship, but the old friends who had loved, supported, and validated me. So I planned a visit to soothe my wounded, insecure self. But the trip was foiled when my "new" 20-year-old car broke down. Crestfallen, I went to visit my mentor at the time and amidst a deluge of tears, threw myself a pity party. I had wanted this so badly, I told her. I had been so excited...

"What's wrong with your car?" she asked pointedly. Somewhat taken aback by the mundane nature of the question, I answered simply; "something with the timing belt." She grinned. "I find it interesting that the *timing* belt is the problem." I didn't understand what she meant, not fully, but looking back years later it was obvious: what I had wanted was validation and love. That want, in and of itself was not the problem. The problem was that I wanted it from *them*. I was looking outside of myself for something I had to first learn to give *to* myself. If I had gone on that trip, I may have gotten the validation I wanted, but it would have been fleeting. It also could have encouraged me to continue to look outside of myself for these things, thereby setting me up to be dependent upon the perception of others to feel good, whole.

In short, I wasn't ready yet – it wasn't *time*. It was a startling realization and a profound lesson.

I still had to fix the timing belt, of course. But the lesson was learned. Now, whenever something in my life isn't working, I don't just ask myself why, I ask myself what I could be trying to learn, what good could come of this situation. I try to find a way to "get it", see the lesson and make the changes in myself.

Change Your *Implied* Self-Talk

Consciously 'tuning-in' and choosing your energy, your vibration, is essential to living a life you'll love. When you are dialed in and monitoring your personal god-force energy, your subconscious can be a positive, affirming, soul-self expression chattering away in your mind. But left entirely to its own devices your subconscious can easily become a voice and perspective riddled with fear, self-doubt, sadness, and anger. Without monitoring and management, your subconscious – and subsequently your energy and vibration - are deeply impacted by your surroundings; the media, friends & family, past experiences, and so on. Even your own self-talk can start to steer your subconscious to the negative.

I'm not talking about your blatant self-talk here... We all know what that is. We've talked about the Alphabet List & there are whole books on the idea in your local bookstore. What I'm talking about here is *implied* self-talk.

Saving It

There is a beautiful, white-ceramic-encased, fountain ink pen on my kitchen table. It's there because I'm not sure where else to put it. I'm not sure where else to put it because it's too nice to put in my desk drawer. It's too nice to put in my desk drawer because I don't want to *use* it... I want to *save* it.

There's a jar of gourmet pesto in my fridge that's under the same, paralyzing spell. When I recently picked up the pen, went through the same cycle of thought and set it right back down where it was, something clicked, and I finally realized how flat-out-crazy it sounded. Why in the world would I need to *save* a pen?? Because it might run out of ink? And what, I'd never be able to afford another pen? Or there would never be a pen that was good enough? I realized I do this in all kinds of ways in my life – in my closet I save the 'good' shirt in case a special event comes up. In my bathroom I 'save' the good towel for – well, for god knows what. In my cupboard, I 'save' the good peanut butter for... when I'm really, REALLY hungry? I don't even know what I'm saving this stuff for! But I did realize that every time I do that, I'm subtly telling myself that there won't be more, that I won't ever be able to buy the good peanut butter or pesto again, that I once that shirt wears out there won't be enough money for a new one, that if I use the good towel, I won't be able to dry myself on anything else... It implies lack. Over and over and over again I'm telling myself this is the best there will ever be and I'd damn well better save it in case there isn't anything more. Ever. What a load. I don't want to be wasteful, I want to be as gentle with the earth and its resources as possible... but if I need to write, I want to use the good pen. There will be another one. If I need to eat, I want to eat the good peanut butter.

Comparing

I was a typical teenager, and spent my youth telling myself I wasn't pretty, I wasn't good enough, I wasn't talented, I wasn't important, there was no way the person I was with could love me, and on and on and on... I spent an embarrassing amount of time worried about how fat I was, how awful my skin was, how ugly and plain and boring I was. I wasn't popular, I wasn't attractive, I wasn't smart, I wasn't talented, I wasn't athletic... but those are not the statements I told myself. What I did tell myself was *how much better everyone else was*. My friends were all so much prettier, so much more athletic, so much more talented, so much smarter, so much more fun, so much more appreciated... So, while I was only occasionally focusing on my own shortcomings, I was PERPETUALLY focusing on how much better they were - which left me feeling as though I 'stacked up' pitifully against them.

Looking back, I can see that even my body was sending me messages about the discord, but I was so tuned out, I didn't recognize them.

I remember how I used to feel when a commercial about, say, acne medication came on television. My chest would tighten, and I'd feel a little angry, a little sad, a little depressed. *Yes*, I'd think as a stunningly beautiful teenager would come on the screen, not a spot on her face, complaining about acne in her 30s. *Yes, it IS terrible isn't it? I am nearly 30 and my skin is a mess and I'm ugly and nothing has changed, and I have tried everything... I'm just not meant to be pretty.* (There was actually a medication that worked... until I had an allergic reaction and a weird abrasion developed on my knee. Seriously. I have a small scar to prove it. I finally had a clear face, but it came with weird spots on my legs. Yep. That's when I realized my body was trying to tell me something. Hint: it wasn't about acne.)

Without realizing it, I let the commercial make me feel ugly. Same thing with weight loss medication. I was never fat, per say… stocky maybe. Still, after an hour of tv and four commercials, I was sure I needed to eat nothing but celery for a week and buy $1000 worth of acne creams I couldn't afford.

It happened in conversations with friends too; as soon as I heard them talking about their partners failings, I was sure I was either failing in the same way, or that my partner was. Out on the town hours later, I'd double down. Or at least my out-of-control-mind would. Suddenly I was sure every woman my partner and I encountered was skinnier, clear-er skinned, and better at relationships than I, better for him than I. That intensely crazy insecurity must have been super attractive. (Insert eye roll here).

It happened in professional contexts; when people mentioned challenges at work, I was reminded I had many of the same struggles and parroted them back to my friends and co-workers - re-enforcing to BOTH of us that we weren't really doing very well, we weren't happy, we weren't in good jobs, and so on. I wasn't necessarily saying bad things, but I was committing another major sin against self-love; I was comparing.

I had stopped monitoring my mental voice and my implied self-talk kept pushing me back into that negative place. When I slowed down and paid attention, I realized that I could be happy for my friends without feeling like they were doing better than I was. Or that I could empathize with and comfort them, without it meaning something was also wrong in my life. I could just celebrate with them or comfort them and STOP THERE. Huh. Light bulb moment.

Comparing yourself to anyone else is pointless. Compare yourself only to the kind of person you want to be.

Criticizing

As we've discussed and most everyone knows, criticizing yourself is a fruitless endeavor and, I believe, self criticism actually programs your brain to believe you aren't worthy of "good" or "wealth" or "love". Just by the sheer power of repetition and suggestion, you begin to believe less of yourself, believe yourself to be wrong, bad, fat, thin, mean... whatever.

Beating back your own criticism of yourself is both a constant practice (at least at first), and absolutely essential. As is reigning in our habit of criticizing and judging others - even *to ourselves.*

On my way across town not long ago, I found myself behind an older vehicle with what appeared to be a very short, silver haired old man in the driver's seat. As I accelerated and braked without ever actually reaching the speed limit, I became aware of the frustration bubbling up inside me. I was on my motorcycle, hovering at that awkward speed between gears where I was going too slow to shift up, but the engine was whining because I was really going too fast for the gear I was in. I couldn't pass him because there was a line of traffic on one side and I couldn't seem to make him hear my silent pleas to just step on it! Just as I began to mentally spew some slew of criticism... I realized what was happening. I felt awful. How was I to know what this person's experience was? Perhaps he'd been in a car accident yesterday and was feeling particularly unsafe. Perhaps he was coming from the vet where he'd just had to put his dog down and was so overcome with emotion he didn't noticing how slow he was moving. Perhaps he had a vase of flowers for his sickly wife in his passenger's seat and was driving really carefully so as not to spill them.

It occurred to me in that moment that even when we silently criticize others, we're still putting out that energy of judgement, negativity, and anger. Which, of course - in this case at least - is likely hurting me and my energy WAY more than it's hurting the old man. But more than that... when we allow ourselves to be critical of others - even just in our own minds - we are normalizing criticism in general and making it that much easier for our brain to go to that "default" setting when we're unhappy. Which just perpetuates the problem and makes criticizing a habit. One that tears us down on all kinds of levels.

Our minds are devoted slaves... of whatever we put into them. They are incredible, powerful computers that will focus on and repeat whatever information we upload into them. So, in order to battle the day-to-day barrage on our spiritual health that is life in this century, we must be ever diligent in re-programming our brains to feed us positive messages and implied "self-talk", stay focused on ourselves, on the good, and especially the good in ourselves.

It is constant work, but it isn't hard. As soon as you hear your mind tell you something negative, re-direct it to something positive. As soon as you feel your chest tighten in fear of something - particularly inadequacy - tell yourself "no" and re-direct that energy to something that feels good and supportive, something affirming and kind. If you catch yourself comparing, judging or criticizing, stop. Bless the other person with love and think about something else.

For example, if you find your mind wandering over to 'Ken and Barbie are happier than we are' or 'Ken and Barbie should be doing this', gently, mentally say "No." or "Stop." and think about something else. Something good. Maybe about yourself, like how successfully you've learned to dance the tango, or how much fun you and Treavor had when the fishing line broke at the lake last fall. Or, go for something different. *Totally different.* Like what a pleasant day it is, or the lovely design on the coffee cup, or how grateful you are for… anything. (Finding something to be grateful for is super easy and really powerful. If you're stuck, always go with gratitude.) It doesn't take long to make your 'default' position one of positive support, affirmation and gratitude instead of inadequacy and negative judgement. Turning off the TV helps too. Practice, though, above all else, will help train your brain to think good things when the impulse is negative and THAT gift alone is incredibly valuable.

I'm now proud to say that not only can I watch tv without a negative emotional response to commercials, I can also feel genuinely thrilled for a friend's success without comparing it to mine, I can listen when they need to talk about their relationship without finding fault in my own, I can even empathize and swap similar stories without quantifying myself as worse or better or anything else.

Sometimes the littlest victories are the biggest ones too.

Tune in to Yourself
Listen to the Universe; You

You. You co creator of all things in your life, you are magnating / attracting / creating whether you realize it or not. That means that when you want or need something, you are putting out the vibration for that thing / person / experience whether you realize it or not. So, when something good - or terrible - happens, stop to understand what messages you may be sending yourself. What your soul-self, higher-self, god-self is telling you.

I literally ask for help, for signs, for information or evidence from the Universe ALL. THE. TIME. Like many times a day. Most of the time I get an answer or a message and most of the time, I follow through on it. Most of the time.

Many years ago, I'd already been thinking about buying a bigger motorcycle for some time when a friend of mine happened to mention she was selling hers. I loved my Buell but I wanted something heavier, with a bigger tank... so I jumped at the opportunity. She dropped it off at my house so I could test ride it when I got home and as I changed into my boots, I sent up a little thought / prayer / intention: *Angels, guides, high beings, god-self... if this bike is meant for me, make it easy, make it obvious. If it's not meant for me, get in the way.* I put my bandana on, grabbed my riding glasses and headed outside.

When I stood next to it, I was reminded how much taller my friend is than I. I swung my leg over the saddle anyway. When my foot dangled several inches from the driveway, I had to shift in the seat to get my foot down so I could bear all the weight on my right leg and stand it up. A situation I don't particularly like. I tipped the bike off its kickstand anyway. Awkwardly balanced on one leg, I reached forward for the custom drag-style handlebars and was reminded my friend was really quite a bit taller than I. I leaned over the tank and started the thing anyway. I felt a little panic when I thought about releasing the clutch, accelerating, picking up my one foot, and heading down the driveway, but I did all of that anyway. I headed up the street anyway. And when it ran out of gas three blocks into the test ride – and on one of the steepest hills in town - I had to wait rescue astraddle the thing to keep it from tipping over because I couldn't reach the kickstand. And as I pushed it down the bicycle lane back toward home… I decided to buy it anyway. I told myself it was just the bike and I getting to know each other.

I had to make three separate trips to the courthouse to get it registered because of paperwork snafus. Titling and licensing cost way more than they should have, the insurance paperwork took forever… but when I finally could, I rode that bike nearly every damn day.

Two months later a family friend mentioned he was selling his girlfriend's bike. It was an Ultra Low. It had less miles. A nicer seat. Better suspension. And it had been impeccably maintained; parked in a heated, show-car garage. (Literally. He had a trophy case in there.) As soon as I test rode it I knew it was the bike that was meant for me.

Because he was a family friend, the guy held 'my' bike for months as I worked to sell the bike I had just bought – for a painful loss – and come up with the cash to re-register and pay taxes on the new bike.

It all worked out in the end, but I could probably have enjoyed more relaxed, blissful, comfortable riding and saved a good chunk of cash if I had listened to the message the Universe – my soul-self – was screaming to me.

You, the Universe, your soul-self, is always sending you messages. Listen, as much as you can, and look for what you need to learn, what your soul might be wanting you to see or experience, what your god-self wants to create. You'll be ok no matter what, things will work out the way they are supposed to, but you might be able to make it easier on yourself if you open yourself up and listen to the messages.

Love Your Everything

If you want financial security, feel financially secure. Imagine it and spend as much time as you can feeling that feeling. Then LOVE the way you spend money. Not just on anything, but on the things you really love. Do you LOVE that pair of jeans? Do you love it $100? Do you love it $100 out of your travel fund, or grocery money, or savings account? You get the idea.

If you want a healthy romantic relationship, be a healthy, romantic person - to yourself. Love the way you imagine feeling in a healthy, romantic relationship. What does it FEEL like? Trust? Joy? Security? LOVE the way you TRUST YOURSELF, the way you ENJOY yourself, your life. Love the secure and freeing feeling of not needing someone. Love the feeling of just enjoying someone.

If you want a beautiful body, love your body. Love the way it feels to have complete and utter confidence. Now LOVE the way you treat your body, LOVE the way you dress your body, tell your body how much you love it.

If you want a nice home, nurture the one you've got. Cleaning the house is a perfect 'nurturing' activity. And, incidentally, it's a great way to show yourself love by nurturing your personal oasis.

No matter what you want in yourself and in your life, choose to love what you already have. Really feel love for the parts of that vision that are already true in your life. Love yourself as much as possible. In every way you can think of, every time you think of it, find something about yourself or the life you've created to love. Love love love love love. Really. It'll change everything.

4

Make Yourself Magic

Ok, we've addressed cleaning and tuning-in to our greatest sensory tool – our bodies. We've discussed monitoring and programming our computers – our minds. We've explored changing our beliefs around our powerful god-selves and owning that power spiritually. Which brings us to this last step.

These are the basic principals, the elements of personality development and daily-life practices that you can use to actively manifest the life you want. This is the point where all those ideal conditions we set up in the previous chapters meet up with the soul-beings we're creating ourselves to be – and that is where the magic happens. At least it did for me.

Gratitude in Perception

Begin with gratitude. Always begin with gratitude. You might be surprised to discover how much of what you think you want, you already have.

To a degree, having what we want is a matter of perspective. I can't count the number of times I've decided I want to create something and as I clarify my desire further and further, I realize I already have what I want in some measure - I just want more of it. Confidence, for instance. Or

---

79

financial security. Or freedom. So, I start focusing on how good what I already have makes me feel, and then swell that feeling with even more gratitude. I FEED the feeling with gratitude for what I already have.

Gratitude is a great tool to help you begin to magically manifest the life you want, because it's quite likely you are already living that life to some degree. Focusing on what you already have will only bring more, help you more powerfully identify with the *feeling* you are really after, and can help you bring into focus new ways what you want can be – *or already is* – manifested in your life. In the case of money, for example... Perhaps you want to travel more. Instead of bemoaning the financial lack that keeps you from booking that ticket, find gratitude for the home you're able to rent or buy, the car you are driving, the bills you are paying on time, and so on. It's possible that through this exercise you realize that you are grateful for the $10 you have to spend on lunch every day. Oh, and wait. If you forgo lunch "out" for a few months, you would save a few hundred bucks and could take your trip. It is also possible that all that gratitude "magically" manifests in a few hundred bucks gifted to you in some way. (But don't focus on HOW it will come. Just feel the gratitude for what you already have, and the gratitude for how it will feel in the near future when you book those tickets.)

Or maybe you want a better relationship. Turn it around with gratitude for the good you have with your partner, and you may see a quick change - not because you manifested a different relationship or somehow manipulated your partner to change into the person you think they should be... but because you realize they really are wonderful exactly the way they are - even in their flaws. Choosing to see them as the supportive, kind, caring, loving, funny, playful, curious (or whatever) individual they truly are (instead of seeing them as 'wrong') will help you see them as a wonderful partner. Perhaps even exactly the kind of partner you want in your life. And you'll only recognize, appreciate, and really FEEL more of those good qualities by investing some grateful attention on the amazing partner you already have. It's easy to focus on the flaws and the faults. But it's just as easy to focus on the good. And when you are joyful (grateful, patient, kind) your partner will likely feel your appreciation, and your positivity and gratitude will become contagious.

Or you might realize you don't have as much to be grateful for as you'd hoped. In that case, maybe it isn't the right relationship, or job, or whatever. Even still; being grateful for the good things in your current situation may help you exit the relationship or circumstance more easily – if that's your choice - and ensure the next person or opportunity or whatever has all those great qualities too.

So first find gratitude. For everything you have. And the inevitable manifestation of the future you so desire.

Gratitude in Action

Since our minds dutifully parrot the thoughts we've (intentionally or unintentionally) programmed and "tune us in" to whatever energy we're feeling… living in a constant state of gratitude will only bring more to be grateful for. In part, because the exercise of focusing on what you're grateful for inherently brings to the forefront of your mind all the good in your life - which reverberates through your body as the energy of all that good… how it FEELS to have all that good - and that dials you in to that particular vibrational frequency, connecting and attracting more of all that good. If you want more money, be grateful for the money you have. Even if it's just a couple pennies you found under the couch cushions. Especially if it's just a couple of pennies.

One of the incredible masters in my life once suggested a very valuable practice for orienting toward gratitude - particularly in the context of money. She told me to pick up every coin I found on the sidewalk and give thanks for the bounty of the universe I was gifted. Of course, I couldn't imagine collecting these coins would, in and of itself, create the life of financial freedom I so desired (though perhaps if I'd stumbled upon a really rare one or something it may have), but I got the point. I began doing this and within just a couple of months, my financial "luck" began to change. A friend called me to design her website and another asked me to blog for her business. And more opportunities continue to come.

Now every time I get a check, or someone buys my lunch, or I find a penny on the sidewalk I send up a silent message of gratitude. And I take a moment to really feel it. I get giddy. I celebrate. I throw my arms (real or imagined) up in the air and give thanks.

This idea of gratitude – and perhaps just as importantly, *acceptance* - changed the way I operated socially too. As a 'good girl', I had been taught all my life to reject gifts. At least once or twice. It's the socially appropriate thing to do. But doesn't it sound ridiculous? If someone wants to give you a gift, why would you reject it? The only reason I can conceive to explain this behavior, is based on an assumption that the recipient has somehow decided the giver isn't authentic or genuine and is giving out of guilt or duty. Which doesn't make them very awesome. And it makes ME even less awesome for thinking that of them. And, how could we ever know that? And isn't it kind of demeaning to first assume that we know the intention and then assume we know the intention stems from guilt or obligation? Doesn't rejecting the gift also imply "I'm so good / wealthy I don't need your gift?" Isn't that kind of pretentious too?

I remember how actually bad it felt – to truly want the gift and feel as though I had to reject it. To essentially tell someone I loved or respected that I didn't want their generosity or kindness. The further I explore the idea, the more genuinely crazy it sounds. I can't believe it took me as long as it did to realize it wasn't doing anyone any good.

After some consideration, I also realized that in my case, at least, a part of the resistance was also my feeling that accepting a gift was somehow an acceptance of charity, that taking their gift suggested that I couldn't give something like that to myself. How ridiculous! Of course someone offering to buy my dinner was not making an effort to take care of me or suggesting I couldn't feed myself… it was a gift. And my sensitivity and resistance were – of course – just my own insecurity and habit of perpetuating lack. You'd think that since I was flat broke and asking the Universe for financial support every day, it would be clear to me that these offers were the UNIVERSE – my powerful soul-self – taking care of me. GIFTS! Not only a gift from my friend, but a gift from the Universe.

I will admit that it still feels very awkward and socially 'wrong' to just accept a gift right out of the box. But I'm trying to just smile, accept with DEEP and sincere gratitude, and wholeheartedly express my thanks.

The same principals – both in my history of rejection and my efforts to accept - are true with compliments. For years, people around me were trying to build me up, trying to reflect back to me the images of myself I had been working so hard to believe, and I was REJECTING them! I was telling people over and over that if they thought I looked nice, they were either wrong, or it was just the lighting. Literally, I think I said that a couple times; "The lighting in here makes everybody look good." If they told me I was talented I said "No, no! No... just lucky." Did you hear that? When people told me I was talented, I said "No." So stinking crazy.

I still have to practice accepting – gifts and compliments – and it still feels awkward, but I'm getting better at it. I just say "thank you" as sincerely as I can and try to let myself really feel the gratitude for a moment, really feel the compliment, appreciate the gift.

This practice was especially useful when I was at a point in my life where I really had to scrimp and save to get the money together for even the most basic things and that has helped me find gratitude more easily - especially when I "have" to spend money, like on the electric bill. Or rent. When I have to put tires on my car, for instance, I make sure that I am FULL of gratitude. When I leave the tire store, I tell myself over and over how grateful I am that I am able to afford good tires, that I'm so glad I can feel safe. I remind myself how thankful I am that I feel especially confident on snowy roads. I acknowledge the time in my life when I couldn't afford a car at all and I find even more gratitude that I had the money to put tires on the one I've got.

I do this kind of exercise for almost anything I can imagine. I put extra effort into it when it's something I didn't necessarily want but rather "had" to buy, and I find as many reasons as I can to be grateful that I have this thing to do at all.

Honesty

Make your word TRUTH. Even to yourself. PARTICULARLY to yourself. When you are finding good things to say about yourself, wonderful things to focus on in your reality, find things that your brain has already decided are really there - even if they look a little different. If you are focusing on how successful you are, for example, keep your speech truthful and find a place in your life where you already feel like a success – and then "amp up" that feeling.

Making your word truth in your own mind helps your computer believe what you tell it, and it helps you believe in yourself. If your word is always truth, *your* truth, when you tell yourself you are abundantly wealthy or deeply loved it's easier to resonate with those feelings. If you see yourself as abundantly wealthy and choose to FEEL abundantly wealthy because you can afford to go to the movies this weekend, it's true. You will also be "abundantly wealthy" when you can go to Belize this weekend.

Speak About - and Focus on – the Good

Perspective, as we've discussed, is such a powerful thing and focusing on the good will only bring more good, deeper and more genuine feelings of gratitude and well being, and on and on and on. So, CHOOSE to see – *and speak about* – the good things as much as possible.

I originally struggled with this idea particularly in conversation; of course I wanted to be honest with my friends and family, keep my word truth - but I also wanted to create a "better" reality than the one I was living. I wanted to speak as though I already had the success I was working to create, but I also wanted to be honest. It took a little practice, but it didn't take long for me to realize there is a way to do both. In fact, I realized that I had been doing it all along, but backwards; I was always choosing the negative side. For instance, when a friend or family member asked me how work was going I often said "Good," and proceeded to follow that up with a statement like "Slow, but good," or "It could be better, but good," or "I'm not quite 'there' yet, but it's coming." I felt wrong somehow saying "good", or even "really good".

When I explored the emotion further, I realized I felt guilt – as though I didn't deserve the success. And I felt like it wasn't enough… even when I was earning more than I ever had and doing more of what I loved. But in truth, work *was* going well. Really well, even. Still I *did* want more success, more books sold, and more clients.

Over and over again I was telling anyone who asked that "good" didn't actually mean "good", that it actually meant that I wasn't quite "making it". All I had to do was drop the second half of the statement. Or, better yet, find something else to focus on. "Good! I'm writing like crazy!" Yes, I was writing because I wanted to instead of for paying assignments, but that didn't matter. I realized it was true, and I felt better about myself saying it that way. Not only that, but focusing on the good sent a positive, high energy vibration out there about my work life, and even better, one that was reflected back and reinforced by everyone I told because *they* thought of my career as "Good!" and my work as "Writing like crazy!" I spoke truth, I THOUGHT truth - to myself and about myself - and that helped my brain realize I was already a success, which made it easier to imagine and visualize myself as even more successful.

Today, those statements are truer still. I "need" less and am creating more. I had to take some time to work on believing I deserved my success, and I had to really focus on how successful I already was. Once I did, it helped me move through the "stuck" energy of lack I had been creating.

One of my most cherished mentors mentioned the way she also used these kinds of interactions as opportunities to celebrate her success, keep her word as truth, AND help manifest more. When someone asked her about how work was going, she responded, "Good! I'm busy!" It didn't matter that often she was busy doing paperwork, planning classes and workshops, or just working to manifest more clients - she *was* busy.

Love the way you think and speak about your life.

Focus Your Truth on the Good

Years ago, I took a part-time position in an office to help make ends meet. The boss was a micro-manager and his obsession with perfection and minute details often translated into barbed conversations with his staff and a generally abrasive professional personality. I had been warned of this when I first began work there; the other people on the team reminded me to have "thick skin". As I have always been a particularly sensitive soul, the first few times I was criticized in front of the team I was both angry and hurt, and immediately felt myself wanting to run. Still, I liked the staff and the work, and the money was absolutely necessary at the time. So, I challenged myself to a different perspective. Every morning in my meditations I would take an extra moment to see my boss surrounded in warm, bright, white light. I saw him smiling. I asked the Universe to bless him with love, fill him with love, FLOOD him with love. I mentally listed out several of the things I liked and admired most about him. When I was at the office, I practiced talking with co-workers about the things I respected in him, the things I was learning from him, and so on. Almost immediately I felt my reactions to him change. But the really incredible thing came a couple of months later when a co-worker and I went out for a glass of wine after work one night. My new friend talked a bit about her personal struggles with the boss and then said offhandedly, "It's actually been a lot better since you started." I didn't say anything of course, and there could have been a lot of other factors at play, but I took it as a sign that my effort to see the good in our boss was helping to draw the good out of him, or help my co-workers see the good in him. Or, at least, create a little nicer office environment.

I realize that sometimes finding the good can be hard. Life is full of challenging situations, people... even certain ideas and beliefs can be abrasive. Look for the good anyway. There's always some there and changing the way you perceive and feel about the situation will change your reality. Acknowledging the difficult is valuable – it can help us grow. But don't wallow there. The waters of the ocean pull back from the beach before rushing forth in a wave of wonder. Believe the same in your life; the challenges that seem to pull you "backward" may simply be the shift before the surge of good that propels you forward.

Choose to see and feel true love for the good things - and the challenges - in your life.

Take Credit

I am in no way suggesting bragging, ego stroking, or anything of the like. What I'm talking about here is the way you represent yourself to the outside world. Tell your friends and neighbors that you are doing well, and that you deserve it, and that you have been working for it. Not so blatantly as all that, perhaps, or it may come off as a little self-indulgent, but take credit for the work you've done and the successes you've realized.

Talk about the success YOU created, and the struggles. Mention what you are learning from the challenges in your life instead of complaining about what is happening "to" you. Of course, you may want to vent your feelings to a close friend or romantic partner but work to spend the vast majority of your thoughts and speech on the ways you OWN your own life.

Years ago, at a time of major transition in my life, I chose a path that required me to find a new place to live. In my meditation one morning I spent some time imagining my new home and asked the Universe for exactly what I wanted; a house with a fireplace, a yard, and a garage, in my favorite neighborhood. When I picked up the classifieds that day, I called the first ad listed under the neighborhood section I dreamed of, and went to see the house later that day. My breath caught in my throat as I mounted the stairs. It was beautiful, though a little big, with a gorgeous old fireplace in the center of the living room and a perfect sized yard in the back for my pup. The property manager told me the rent would be significantly reduced for some time while they converted the old play space back to a garage. I could hardly believe it! I signed the lease an hour later. And then I worried over it. I could afford it, but I felt guilty about it somehow... maybe for my environmental impact, maybe for living in a nice house when I knew people who weren't able to make smaller payments... When people complimented me on the house, I dodged it; "It's not as big as it looks," or "It's nice but there are lots of problems."

Eventually I realized that I was giving away all of my power. Yes, the house was bigger than I needed - but it was also so close to downtown that I could ride my bike three seasons of the year to meetings, walk to dates with friends, and so on. Also, I closed off the basement, made it a storage space for a couple of friends in transition, and just used the upper two floors. And I had always been particular about where and how I spent my money; on things that mattered to my heart, from local people and businesses that I respected, and in donations to organizations I believed in.

The point was I didn't need to feel guilty – especially in front of myself – about where I lived. I deserved to give myself some of that support and put the money I had earned into a place where I LOVED living. I deserved to take credit for the life I'd worked for, the life I'd created. That put some of the guilt to rest.

Then I addressed the big one, the deeper one; my guilt about my success. Why in the world should I feel guilty? My success was not directly connected to the lack of another.

Just because I was successful didn't mean that money was coming out of the grocery budget of a needy family. In fact, quite the opposite. When I have the financial freedom I want, I spend more to shop locally. I could even get excited about spending $20 more on shoes at the family-owned outdoors store because my purchase may have helped them buy quality food or pay the rent on their child's band instrument. I wanted to be proud of my success. I had worked hard for it. I had earned it. And I realized as I went through the process that I had been downplaying my success for years! I felt guilty for it, for taking credit for what I'd earned. No wonder I had struggled with it for so long! I felt guilty every time I mentioned something *I* associated with financial success and I realized I felt guilty talking about my house or my vacation plans or whatever with my friends. I had no reason to feel guilty. But there it was. When I realized I hadn't been owning my power or allowing myself to be proud of my own success, I realized I needed to change that. I began telling myself "I am proud of my success," or "I deserve a nice home," every time I felt guilty. I reminded myself that having wealth would allow me to share it – perhaps even in some small way helping someone else - and that my success didn't take success away from someone else. In fact, in my belief system, money is just a tangible expression of energy and love... so having more money just meant I had a different iteration of the energy and love I already had. My success just meant that I had more to share.

Every time I caught myself trying to downplay my life to my friends, I worked to feel humble gratitude and just answer honestly instead; "Yes, business is great! Thank you!"

Use Your Body

Our bodies are tremendous energy-sensing tools. In fact, they are THE energy sensing tool. Not your mind.

I was recently reminded of the power in our bodies by a scientist who encouraged everyone who heard the message to share it, so I will do so here. But I'll leave the science-y stuff to the scientists. In a nutshell, standing with your arms up, as in a show of victory, or with you hands on your hips and feet apart, as in the Wonder Woman stance, for two minutes, literally changes the hormones in your bloodstream and positively impacts your ability to believe in yourself, exhibit and command confidence and therefore success. So now, whenever I'm about to face something difficult, or if I'm feeling weak, vulnerable, insecure or whatever... I take two minutes to stand in "power stance". Since two minutes can feel like forever when you're just standing, I also use the time to go through the alphabet list. It's a great way to help my brain - and my body - feel my confidence, my power, and FEEL the energy I want to have in my life.

Feel

In the world of energy, thinking is powerful. Largely, because a thought inspires a feeling in your body, creating a "loud" vibrational frequency that becomes a powerful magnet for similar frequencies and therefore similar experiences. Thinking gratitude when you find a penny on the sidewalk *will* have an impact on your energy, your vibration. But taking an extra moment to FEEL that gratitude will supercharge that vibration. The same is true for love, and for joy, and for peace… and for fear, and hate, and anger. Focusing on those things… particularly on how those things FEEL, brings more of those feelings into your life. In those moments when you feel fear, anger, sadness, or any other feeling you'd like to change… just change. Change anything. Change what you're doing at the moment - turn on the radio, perhaps, or pick up a book or a deck of cards… anything to distract your mind. When the negative thought or emotions have passed, take a moment to focus on the good, FEEL the gratitude for whatever good has come - because there's ALWAYS something good - and let *that* feeling bubble over in you. Bring the good, the lesson, into sharper focus and FEEL the wide array of potential positive impacts - it may just help you move through the 'negative' faster.

And, since your mind is constantly picking up cues from your surroundings, give it cues that make you feel good – in general. Surround yourself with images that inspire you, especially if they also remind you of your dreams and goals. Play music that makes you smile or want to dance along. Fill your home with textures you love, art you love, smells you love. Choose positive and joyful content on TV and radio to fill your mind. Keeping a clean home, too, will help. Cluttered or dirty surroundings can often inspire feelings of chaos and disharmony. A clean, organized space that feels like your personal sanctuary will help to keep you feeling calm and optimistic.

Feel your way through tough decisions and situations. Find stillness and quiet, and then try to feel your body react to people, ideas, and opportunities. Your body will tell you what your heart already knows.

Act it Out

How do your clothes feel? How do they make *you* feel? Do you feel like they align with the version of yourself you want to create? Do they feel like the clothing a successful designer might wear? Or like the clothing a mother of three might wear? Or the clothing the VP of Operations might wear? There's wisdom in that old idea of 'dressing for success' – as long as you keep true to yourself. Dress the way you imagine YOU will want to dress when you've manifested what you want. ACT the way you imagine YOU will act. EAT the things you imagine YOU will eat in the role / place / reality you want to create. Try on 'being' the you that you really want to be. Do you walk or drive in your dream-life? Do you drink coffee or tea? Do you visit libraries on your lunch hour or shopping malls? Spend a Saturday acting like you are already 'there' and see how it feels. When it feels amazing try doing it more often. Walk around your life like you're already living the 'dream' version.

Visualize

As elements of god, creators of our own realities, we use our brains to "sketch out" the versions of reality we choose. Intentionally or unintentionally, we are constantly feeding our brains with information - pictures, words, ideas, sounds, smells, feelings - about our realities, about what they look like. So, as creators, when we want something different, it is our job to give our slave-computer minds OTHER information about our realities.

If we can simulate the realities we want, we can more easily connect with - and therefore "create" - them in the physical world. All manner of professionals; Business People, Athletes, Practioners... use visualization techniques to "get their heads right" or program their brains to respond in certain ways, therefore creating certain outcomes.

Visualization techniques are encouraged by psychologists and life coaches, therapists and trainers, to help their clients create different (better) versions of themselves or their circumstances from the wide array of possible realities that exist in any given moment of time.

So why not you?

Many, many great minds have touted the benefits of visualization for all kinds of things and there's a reason it is used as widely as it is - from athletes to business coaches - because it works. Visualize whatever you want to create in your reality. Just take a few minutes every day. EVERY DAY. Focus your brain on what you want to create and see how it looks, but even more importantly, see how it FEELS. Let yourself FEEL wealthy; feel the joy of booking tickets for your next vacation, or the joy of a fridge full of good food, or the general relaxation of financial security, or the joy of paying bills. (Personally, I LOVE to pay my bills in full and on time... when that screen pops up that says "paid in full"... oh, so full of gratitude! I can pay my bills!!) FEEL loved, FEEL healthy, FEEL beautiful, FEEL joyful... anything and everything. Tactile things too, of course, are manifested this way. If you want a certain thing, imagine yourself holding it, touching it. Describe to yourself the color, the texture, the smell. And FEEL it. Not just the thing itself, but feel how YOU feel holding it, touching it, having it in your life. FEEL it. Vibrate the way you want by FEELING the way you want. Visualize with FEELING and you will see what you want manifested in your life.

Permit me another personal story, this time, from my sister.

Back when we were both quite young; adults in the literal sense but just learning how to really live that way, driving junker cars and living in questionable studio apartments... she got her heart set on a certain kind of vehicle; a Chevy Tahoe. When she told me about this wish of hers, I was excited to suggest some of the new techniques I'd learned in manifestation; visualization, joy, and *feeling*. We talked a lot about how the car would look – inside and out - about how she would feel driving that car, how she would feel coming out of work & getting in that car, how she would feel picking up and dropping off her friends... Her credit wasn't good, and she wasn't making much money at the time... I think we both expected it to take a couple months – a couple weeks at least. But just a few days later, she called me from the loan trailer at a city-wide car sale. She'd been approved and would soon be driving off in the car of her dreams, the color she wanted, the interior she'd dreamed of... she was thrilled. And scared. And thrilled. We talked, she settled into excited, and loved driving that car for several more years. She also became a believer in the power of visualization and manifestation.

Incidentally, FEELING and visualization are also great ways to help yourself make a choice and move forward if you - like I - are the kind of person who sometimes is paralyzed by decision making. When I have a big choice to make, particularly if I really keep fence-hopping, I ask myself "what does my heart want to do"? I take a moment, calm down, clear my mind and then imagine myself making first one

choice and then the other, focusing on how the choice FEELS
- in my body, in my heart, and in my mind. Sometimes, when I
am particularly worked up about a decision, I find it
challenging to feel clearly. I've learned that is just a sign that I
have too much fear or worry involved, and I gently talk my
mind down from the worry-ing ledge, sit back and relax, and
then try to feel again. From a totally neutral place, perfectly
calm, I imagine myself already a ways down each of the paths
I see in front of me as related to this choice.

Remember that house I mentioned loving so much? I'd
been living there awhile when the landlord decided to sell. I
wasn't sure I wanted to buy a house. But I wasn't sure I
wanted to leave either. I went back and forth a million times. I
analyzed, compared and contrasted, looked around for what
else was available... and after all of that, I still had no idea
WHAT I wanted to create in terms of my housing situation. I
didn't even know what I wanted - how could I find or manifest
it?

So, I went to my meditation place, lit my incense, and
got quiet. I told my mind to rest, and then asked for help
from the high beings of the Universe. I stated my intention for
the practice; to find out where my heart wanted to live, and
then made my mind blank. I took some deep breaths, and
first I imagined myself renting another house. Any other
house. I imagined making breakfast in a different kitchen, or
having friends over to a different back yard, writing in a
different room... and I felt my body tighten up, I felt a little
sad. I even had a sense of cloudy-ness or darkness come over
me. Then I imagined buying a house - but not this one. It felt
a little better, but still a little grey. Last, I imagined buying this
house and instantly I felt like the sun had been turned on in
my mind. My head and heart were filled with images of light

and playfulness and joy... Which actually surprised me a little because I had no idea how or even if I could buy this house. Turns out, I can.

Imagination – visualization - is a powerful way to connect to your deep self. It can help you determine what you want and see and feel yourself having it. Imagining what success looks and feels like, what happiness looks and feels like, what peace looks and feels like, what love looks and feels like has helped me in untold ways. When I've imagined success as feeling appreciation for my work, I've had people approach me with praise and gratitude. Usually within days. When I've imagined success as financial freedom, I've had new projects and ideas come to me quickly. The same has been true in most every other area of my life.

Love the way you see, the way you act out, the way you imagine your life.

Write it Down

There is a particular process that happens in our minds when we convert thoughts to symbols, and then those symbols to ideas, and back again. It is an incredibly powerful tool. Particularly if you read what you've written. Aloud.

Take some time to write down what you want. No, really. Take some time. Don't rush this process. It can be a surprisingly effective way to help clarify the real essence of your vision, your goals, your dreams. You may find that while you thought you knew exactly what you wanted in a particular area of your life, you aren't as clear on the idea as you imagined. Maybe you know you want to create wealth. But what does that look like to you? Do you want a small house and lots of money to travel? Or do you want to stay home in a house built like a castle? Do you want money to buy fancy clothes or food? Or do you want lots of money to build a wilderness center?

Dream of the life you want, the end goals, and write it down. Explore the feeling that you are really after; the true root of this desire. By that I mean, do YOU really want it? Does your SOUL SELF really want it? Or do you think you need it because societally it represents something *else* you want; love, success, validation, security, joy? Do YOU really want it or is it something a parent or partner or friend once wanted you to want?

For instance, most of us want wealth. But the reasons we want money are as varied as the people who want it. Some want it because it represents freedom. Others because it represents security. Figure out what you want. What you REALLY want. Don't judge it as good or bad, right or wrong. (In my mind, there is nothing inherently wrong with wanting things. The wrong-ness comes in wanting those things to define you. Why do you want what you want? Does it really serve a purpose in your life, or do you want it because you think it will make you look a certain way in front of others? If you want money for validation, find personal attributes to be proud of, to focus your self-worth on.) If you want a romantic relationship, decide how you want your relationship to feel, and how you want to feel in your relationship.

Write it down. Then visualize and FEEL what having these things will be like. Feel yourself having what you want - what you REALLY want. Freedom, security, love, affection, value, respect... whatever it is, find a way to feel it.

Now read your list out loud.
Write it, read it, and then give YOURSELF the feeling.

Love the way your ideal life feels.

Mantras

When one of my friends was going through perhaps the hardest time in her life, when nothing was stable or sure, and she wanted to start moving forward but had no idea where to begin, she started singing to herself.

This beautiful woman had moved halfway across the country to be with the man she loved, truly her soul-mate, only to have him die tragically a few years later. She left her call-center job and their shared apartment behind to come home to her family, but as the dust cleared, she found herself with no career, no partner, no home, no money, and absolutely no idea what she wanted or where she wanted to go - much less how to begin. So, she started singing. She laughed when she told me about it, musing on how funny she must look to passersby, driving down the road, dancing in the driver's seat and "singing"; "Abundance, abundance, abundance." "Joy, joy, joy." She had a special little tune and everything.

Her story stuck with me because I was so impressed with her bravery, her openness to what the Universe could bring, how it could be brought, and the beautiful simplicity of her mantra. Abundance. Joy. The only two things she knew for sure she wanted.

I adopted her effort at musical manifestation when I was going through one of my own "where do I go / what do I do now" moments in life, with a few little tweaks; "Peace. Freedom. Adventure. Love. Luxurious Wealth. Joy." In my head, it rhymes, sort of, and it makes it easy to remember.

I think of her often, particularly when I am not sure what I want, but I know I want a change, or when I can't get the negative thoughts out of my head. Every time I do, I repeat my own mantra, over and over again. "Peace. Freedom. Adventure. Love. Luxurious Wealth. Joy." I say it over and over and over again until my mind is no longer spinning with fear, negative thoughts, judgement, anger, or whatever. "Peace. Freedom. Adventure. Love. Luxurious Wealth. Joy." It always helps me to calm down, focus on the good, dream of what I want - what I *really* want, what my soul-self, my god-self wants - see and feel the ways I already have it, or it's already on its way, and let go of the rest.

Over time I've also used my mantra as a way to conjure up the FEELINGS I want to feel. I slow the mantra down, take it word by word, and create a mental picture. I try to really sink into the way it would FEEL to have peace in every aspect of my life. World peace. Personal peace. Family peace. Then I create a picture of freedom. My freedom. Then I create one for Adventure, and so on. I have also imported this mantra and its associated images and feelings into my morning meditation. Just at the end, I spend a couple of minutes going through my mantra word by word, creating and re-creating the images, and feeling the feelings. It both focuses my thoughts and sends a powerful energetic charge out into the world to help me create all those things in my life.

Trust Your Powerful God-Self

There are infinite ways you will create what you want – so let them be infinite. While using specific examples to clarify how financial freedom FEELS, for instance, focusing too much on the specifics can become "focusing on the 'hows'" and create a block. If you only see one way to achieve financial freedom, you're keeping yourself from getting it any other way. Instead, focus on the end goal, the ultimate feeling. There is an element of trust required in this practice, trust that the Universe (read: YOU) will attract the things you want in a way that will work for you - because it's YOU.

This point was brought home for me several years ago. I had been struggling financially for years. LOTS of years. Like, decades. Even as I learned more and more manifestation techniques and had greater and greater successes with them, I continued to struggle with money.

I worked to re-focus on the good feelings; every time I felt the weight of fear, sadness, or worry about my financial reality, I repeated a mantra. While I don't remember the exact words, I do know it was long and cumbersome and complicated. Something like "I choose to create and accept wealth of $50,000 per year or more, using my gifts and talents, doing work I love, part-time, and in a manner that gives me freedom and complete control of my schedule."

I remember how "tight" it felt... trying to remember all the conditions, trying to imagine all the possible outcomes and predict any "loopholes" I might have missed. Then, one night when I was feeling rather exhausted by the whole thing, the looming payments I didn't have the money for, the complicated way I needed the Universe to bring me what I asked for, I realized; I was behaving as if the Universe were conspiring AGAINST me! How ridiculous is that? One of the first things I learned about manifestation was the importance of believing the Universe was working in your favor. Of course it is... the Universe is YOU! I didn't need to worry about all the ways I could possibly make money and try to direct the Universe to bring it to me a certain way. I already had my own vibration, my "vibe". (Another perk of true self-love and understanding.) I was just adding to that energy by focusing on wealth. The Universe wouldn't bring me a job programming computers to create the money I wanted because it wouldn't match with me energetically anyway. I have no love for computer programming. (Though I do have a deep love for several incredibly talented computer programmers. You see the distinction.) Right then and there, I decided on a number that I wanted to create every month. A dollar amount. And I let the rest of it go. It felt so much better, so much more open, and it felt good to trust that the Universe would bring me what I wanted in a way that worked for me. Of course it would - the Universe was ME! And it's you too.

When I first began visualizing the money - the actual money - I realized I felt some kind of barrier. So, I stopped, I imagined the barrier as a wall and, not even knowing what it was, I saw the wall dropping. Then I imagined the money pouring in. Since one of my financial goals was also to get out of debt and improve my credit score, I also imagined a fuzzy, pink, 790 credit score. I imagined it as fuzzy and pink so I could imagine how it felt to hold it, how it felt to LOVE my credit score. Within weeks my whole financial reality began to change. Over the next year I had many new income opportunities come into my life, new clients, my books were selling like crazy, and I was able to make big payments on my debts.

All that good stuff is still happening today. I've increased the number I imagine flowing in to me every morning in my meditations, and I no longer feel the barrier, so I no longer imagine the wall dropping, but my financial future is very bright. (And guess what my credit score is.)

Trusting my soul-self has delivered things into my life I had never considered wanting. Even as opportunities for financial security began to come into my life, I still didn't really know what I wanted, what I REALLY wanted in terms of my professional definition. I didn't know what the "finish line" would look like. I wanted to write, that much I was sure, but I had no further direction or goal. When a friend approached me one day and asked me to edit his book, I was a little hesitant; I'd never edited anything before, I'm not even a trained editor, I hadn't gone to college for writing or journalism… me? An editor? But I was interested, so I told him all of that, and told him if he still wanted me to do so, I'd look at his book.

I loved it. Not just the book – though that was good too – but the process, the creativity, the discussion on perspective and plot lines. I found myself ecstatic to get back to reading his book, ecstatic to edit and encourage and help draw out the story he was telling. I had never considered editing, but I genuinely loved it.

A few months later, I was asked to be the editor for an arts and entertainment tab of a local newspaper, and I loved that too. That adventure spawned another one: magazine editor. Today I am the Editor-In-Chief of an arts and entertainment magazine and I'm thrilled about it. I never would have considered these paths, but my soul-self, my god-self opened them to me perfectly.

These new opportunities feel to me as though the "threads" of my professional paths are coming together in a beautiful tapestry of purpose. I can now see how the art and event gallery I opened years ago with a friend – that ultimately failed – actually laid the groundwork for my connection with the arts community. I can see how the desire I've long felt to celebrate other people, remind them how amazing they are, has fed my ability to write their stories. I can see how my years of experience in these realms has culminated in yet another beautiful manifestation of my current career path.

The important caveat here is that you are radiating the energy of your true self. Your soul self. Happily, that is a natural state of being when you deeply love yourself. Over the course of my young life I'd manifested several less-than-ideal jobs because I was trying to be someone I wasn't. Or, more accurately, I didn't really know or love who I was. I am so grateful for the teachers who helped me learn to know, love, and trust myself.

Think it, as often as you can. Feel it when you think it. Give your computer - your mind - pictures, and, in moments where you need a quick reminder / validation / mental re-orientation, give it a mantra. A simple one. And then trust your god-self to bring it to you in the perfect way.

Let the Universe give you gifts and just be grateful, as much as you possibly can.

Love the way you trust yourself, your god-self, and flow with the Universe.

Make Change Happen

Do Something Different

Our incredible little computers like habit and dislike change, so one of the most powerful things we can do when we're seeking to change something in our selves or in our lives is to just change. Disrupt the pattern. Break the habit.

Change sparks change. When you feel completely at a loss for anything you can do to move toward the life you want to live or the things you want to create, shake it up. Do something different. Anything. Preferably something out of the ordinary. Draw something cheerful in sidewalk chalk on your front stoop. Visit a flower store. Send a box of chocolates to a friend or stranger. Turn on some music and dance. Go to a matinee. Buy someone a cup of coffee. Change up your routine; have breakfast for dinner, take Wednesday off and work on Saturday, take a class.

Take some time to daydream about a different version of the life you're working toward. Instead of imagining the big bank account, imagine the travel or the donations. Instead of focusing on the relationship you want, focus on the dates you'll go on, the places you might live.

Keep it positive, change it up, and Just. Change. SOMETHING.

Changing your choices, and sometimes your circumstances helps change your thought patterns and habits, and that helps to change your energy.

Move Toward It

What can you do to help bring what you want into your life? What can you do to 'act' like it's already there? Little baby steps can often lead to big changes. So, take a little step.

"Shop" for it. When I first moved into the magic house, I had very little furniture. And what I did have, wasn't particularly nice. I didn't have a lot of money to spend on furniture, in fact I really didn't want to spend ANY money on furniture. But over a long winter I had come to the conclusion that I really did need a better couch. So, I shopped for it. I went online and searched for all the features I was looking for in a couch. I read reviews. I checked out colors, and fabrics and finishes. I decided what I liked and didn't like in terms of style. That spring, my mother and I spent an afternoon shopping for a couch. I found several I liked, but none I loved, and I found myself saying over and over that I wanted a different fabric, or a different size, or a different firmness… I left my mother that afternoon feeling quite happy that I hadn't bought a couch - because I would have bought the WRONG couch.

A few days later, a friend of mine put her couch on an online garage sale. It was exactly the size I wanted, covered in a fabric I didn't know I loved (but I quickly discovered I did), in a color I had never thought of using in my decor (and that coordinated perfectly, I might add), and at a price I could easily afford. When I went to pick it up, she wouldn't even take my money. I had helped her with some things a month or so prior, and she wanted to give me the couch as payment.

Almost the same thing happened when I needed a mirror.

I realized that all that "shopping" for the thing I wanted was just my mind drawing a clearer and clearer picture. It was programming, it was imagining, it was 'trying on' what I needed to find out more clearly what I really wanted. And, importantly, it was an action, a step forward I could take to help bring what I wanted into my life. Now, I consider "shopping" for whatever it is I am hoping to manifest at any given time, an incredible tool. I am careful to keep gratitude in my heart, however… I don't want to focus on the "flawed" versions of what I'm finding when I'm looking. I just keep asking myself over and over again if it is close enough to the most perfect version of the thing I want. And I really do shop for it as though I have all the money in my bag, I just want to spend that money on THE PERFECT one. The one I really LOVE. And now, I almost always manifest exactly what I want - or an even better version I didn't know was available - within a few weeks of deciding I want it.

There are innumerable ways you can begin to take little steps toward the life of your dreams. Hoping to get married? Start planning the wedding. Dreaming of starting a business? Write the business plan. Yearning to travel more? Begin your itinerary. Shopping for a house? Start designing your living room.

Find something you can do that will make you feel like you're already living the early stages of your dream.

Make Space for It

One of the many awkward phases – otherwise known as powerful-growth-phases - of my life occurred when I began to understand that I loved to write. Not the realization itself, but the thought that maybe, I might, by some beautiful chance of the universe, in some magical way, be able to make a living doing this thing I loved. It was awkward because I had not the remotest idea how a person embarks on this kind of thing and so there was much floundering about resulting in several less-than-ideal-for-me jobs. I would come home from work utterly exhausted and thinking to myself "where is *it*?!" I'd been focusing on and dreaming about and imagining and feeling my love for this dream of mine, but it just wasn't coming. When I had the thought that if I just had more time... if I could just win the lottery or be gifted a huge stack of money, I'd have the *time* to be the writer I wanted to be... it hit me. I wanted time. I told myself I had none. And I sat down to watch TV for two hours every night. If I wanted time to do this thing, all I had to do was MAKE the time. So, for the next year or so I pushed myself to get up a half hour early to write. Two years later I quit my traditional job all together. Now I'm a full-time freelancer, event planner, writer, and editor and I LOVE my life. I just had to make space in my routine.

The same concept worked for me in relationships. When I knew for sure I was not in the relationship I wanted I first analyzed whether we weren't a good fit or if I was just so focused on the problems, I couldn't love him for who he really was. Sometimes that process took awhile. Like, years. I first tried to identify how I wanted the relationship to feel. Then, how I wanted to feel in my relationship, and that helped me to see whether or not my partner and I really might work –

whether the lives we wanted would match-up. When that answer became a clear 'no', I knew I had to leave. And sometimes that took awhile. Like, years. In retrospect I'm sure it was fear of being alone, or fear that there wouldn't be anyone better out there, or fear that I was hoping for too much in my romantic partner... but ultimately, the Universe - my god-self - would never be able to bring me the relationship I wanted if I didn't make space for a new relationship in my life... and brave being alone.

Of course, before we go jumping ship in any context of our lives, I believe it is important to know that our decision is coming from our true, deepest heart. The god-self part of us that is never afraid, is never insecure, that never doubts. That part of us that really KNOWS what we truly want, what we're truly capable of, and what we need to do to get it. Sometimes, too, making space for what you want isn't as clear cut as just quitting your job if you want a new one. (Although I've made that work in my life too. But it's usually harder. Sometimes a lot harder.) Often it is important to consider ways that we can make space in our lives for what we want to manifest and work on ourselves in contexts that don't completely disrupt the lives we have. Consider, for example, the desire for a different career. Perhaps instead of just putting in notice with your current employer and then devoting yourself to manifesting money, it would be more well advised to take a class in the field of your dream career. Or, take up a hobby in line with the professional-self you want to create. Or just buy a book on careers in the fields you enjoy.

If you feel there is something creating a block to your growth, make space for change. Get out of the situation or relationship or whatever and look for the love. Find the ways you did - or could have - grown and learned and loved more. Then work to apply those lessons now, so next time you draw someone or something better, higher, and brighter, than you did before.

Make space in your life for the reality you want to manifest.

Create

When you don't know what to do to take action toward your goal or dream or vision… create. Find a way to create something. Anything. Create a cotton-ball snowman, or a pie, or a clothing style, or a sound. Just create. Create messily, create badly. JUST CREATE.

I'm not a good painter. I'm really not. Same goes for crafts of any kind. But I really like to do it. So I do. And I had the thought not long ago that perhaps when we are creating, we are most in touch with our god-selves.

Anytime we make anything - art, music, food - a part of our mind gets quiet and we create from the heart. The ultimate act of the traditional God, too, was 'creation'. And the tremendous and far-reaching positive impact of art in all its forms is well documented. It, too, is the great equalizer; we're all artists in some way. Some of us are terrible painters, and not-so-terrible chefs. Others are incredible photographers, or sculptors, or musicians, or jewelry-makers, or house-painters, or flower-bed-landscapers. There is a creative force in all of us. What if that creative force were a beautiful expression of god force? Nature, even in its flaws - sometimes *because* of its flaws - is beautiful. Art is created to express. Life itself is an act of creation, an *expression* of love. I like the idea, it makes sense to me, it resonates for me. I choose to believe that when we create, we are expressing our god-self. So, create. And see what happens.

Create a Vision Board

Take your time with this, though. Really soak up the experience, taking the time to leaf through travel brochures, for instance, or home design magazines, or parenting publications, or flyers for wealth management. Feel the way it feels to have everything you want. Feel the way it feels to just "order up" the thing you want - the house, the job, the savings account. Choose images that remind you of the way you FEEL. If, for instance, you are working to manifest a home you love, leaf through home magazines or design books and cut out the images that truly spark you. Maybe of families playing games in living rooms, or friends gathered around a table, or people reading by fireplaces. The images that make you gasp a little when you see them or say to yourself "I LOVE that!" or get excited about sharing with your partner. Those are the ones that go on the board.

Love the way you create - anything.

Bring Love

Some time ago, I awoke on a cold, bright winter Saturday morning with a heavy heart. I was living a beautiful life but the world around me seemed to be falling apart and I had been wrestling with the role I was 'meant' to play for weeks. It had been wearing on my spirit, and weighing on my mind, and I felt utterly stuck in the vicious cycle.

   I had planned since the middle of the week to take a hike on Saturday, but had fully intended to stay close to town, and just get out for an hour or so - mostly for the benefit of my dog. But something in me kept whispering, urging me to head south a good hour out of town and spend my outside time in the granite swells and spires that define one edge of the wilderness around my heart's home in the Black Hills of South Dakota. I had also intended to wait for the heat of the day - maybe 32 degrees, if I was lucky. But as I cleaned up the kitchen after breakfast and loaded the dishwasher, I couldn't find excitement or energy for anything but the hike. So, I filled my pack with water and snacks for myself and my faithful companion; a stout little Pit-bull Bloodhound cross with a heart the size of an elephant. She bounded eagerly into the back of my car and an hour later we pulled into the parking lot for a trailhead on the southern edge of the Hills. We were both excited about the adventure but where her joy only grew at the discovery of foot-deep snow covering the trail, mine waned a touch. Ok, it sunk to my shoes. But I was here, and we both needed the exercise, so I pressed on. Within minutes my thighs were aching, but my emotional weight was lifting. So, we pressed on. The bottom half of my pants were soaked with melted snow and the top half of my body was soaked with sweat, but I laughed out loud when I caught sight of my pup, Rumi, heaving herself out of one full-body-snow-print and belly flopping to create another. So, we pressed on. After awhile the fire in my thighs had cooled to smoldering and just as we crested the great granite spine my heart soared. Stretched out in front of us, the dusky blue horizon reached as far as I could see, and a sense of peace washed over me. We trudged on a little further, a little higher up the ridge line and once at the top I stopped for a drink and took a moment to really appreciate my surroundings. The peace and silence of the forest enveloped me. I felt as giant as the pines next to me and, as I gazed out over the landscape, simultaneously as small as the drop of melting snow falling from the pine needles above onto my hat. My place in the Universe was both huge and insignificant. The world would keep turning with or without me. My greatest gift to the world was just to be me, the essence of me; love. I was love. Just love. And all I needed to do was *love*. Bring love. To everything, to everyone. To every thought, every idea, every conversation. There was nothing to judge, nothing to worry about … just bring love.

I accepted that whenever I felt the pressure of fear about something, all I had to do was stop my mind and find a way to love whatever it was that was causing fear. If I felt a twinge of fear about my financial future, I just brought love to my mind and felt it in my heart. Love for my career, love for the money I had, love for the money that I chose to believe was coming, and love for my readers and clients. I chose to feel the love I felt for writing itself. If I found myself worrying about politics or global warming or my family, I just brought love. Love for all those in leadership roles, love for the positions themselves, love for the whole of government, love for the planet, love for the animals, love for tenderness and respect for all things, love for my family members, love for their love of me. Love love love. Just love. However I could find a way to feel it toward any subject or topic, I did. I still do. Every time I find myself fearful, sad, depressed, anxious, worried... I find something to love and I practice BRINGING LOVE.

Believe in Yourself

If you are powerful enough to manifest a positive relationship with your boss, recognize the gift your challenging mother-in-law is giving you, create success for yourself as an artist or a parent or a partner, then you are powerful enough to manifest money or a beautiful home or a new car. You are powerful. You are powerful enough to create anything you want in your life.

Begin with gratitude.
Love yourself completely.
Keep your word truth.
Choose to see the good.
Feel, and listen to your feelings.
Feel what you want to feel.
Visualize.
Write it down.
Give your mind a mantra.
Trust your powerful god-self.
Take action toward your dream.
Pat yourself on the back.
Bring love, to everything. Especially, to yourself.
Give thanks again.

Choose to see the good and you will FEEL more good. Understand that what you perceive to be 'bad' is simply your god-self showing you opportunities for growth, for more love, for greater success, and so on. Complain about the hard things first, if you must, in a safe, protected, closed environment. Then go out and celebrate what you are learning, how you are growing, and give thanks for the challenge-makers in your life because they are only making you more powerful.

Now give thanks again because you are a master manifest-er, an element of god. And give thanks one last time because gratitude for what you have only raises your vibration to have more of what makes you grateful.

First and Last, again and again:

LOVE YOURSELF **MORE**

Love the way you think, the way you eat, the way you talk to yourself, the way you create, the way you spend your time, the way you laugh, the way you learn, the way you tell stories, the way you believe, the way you treat people, the way you take care of your body, the way you exercise… the way you treat YOURSELF… and you will draw to you all you want and need, and more.

Find a way to love, everything and everyone… and LOVE YOURSELF MORE.

What if it isn't Working

Troubleshooting

First, love yourself more. Period. Love yourself more. Do things that feed your *soul*. Spend more time outside. PLAY more. Treat life as a beautiful choose-your-own-adventure and as much as possible, do things you LOVE, do things that make your heart soar. Need some ideas? Draw, paint, sing, dance, exercise, cook healthy things, pick flowers, make music, write poetry, take a bath, go swing at a playground, build sandcastles, make something, play "I spy", invite friends over for a board game, play cards, build a birdhouse, paint your living room, go camping, stay in a bed and breakfast, take a nap in the sunshine, invite someone over for coffee, walk through a greenhouse, send a card to a loved one, visit strangers in the hospital, mow your neighbors lawn or bring them flowers, plant a tree, draw on the sidewalk with chalk, take a stained-glass-window-making class, read a book, cut fun pictures out of magazines, re-organize your closet (don't laugh, that is fun for some of us!), bake some treats and give them away, volunteer at a homeless shelter, go on a photo-hunt... the list is quite literally endless. Do something that makes your soul-self FEEL good, that makes you proud of yourself, something you would do with - or for - someone you dearly loved. Do it for yourself.

Accept responsibility. Quite likely the reason you aren't getting what you are working so hard for (energetically, at least), is because you aren't fully aligned with your true self. There's something in your belief system, in your physical reality, in your self-talk... that is polluting, or re-routing, your energetic focus or flow. Take some time, get in there, and really understand what it is that's getting in the way. Even if you can't quite understand it, acknowledge it and Let. It. Go.

As I mentioned earlier, in my quest to manifest a more secure financial future for myself, I struggled a lot with money. And, while I didn't ever quite pinpoint exactly what the block was (though I suspect it was some guilt for having what others didn't, or the perceived "evil" that I saw in *some* people who were quite wealthy), all I had to do was imagine the block as a wall, and then see the wall falling as I worked to visualize wealth and the wealth came-a-rushing. Seriously. Rushing.

I believe a part of the reason for this is that in visualizing the wall falling, I drew to myself the people and experiences I needed to clear the block, whatever it was. I had the chance to see what the blocks could be; guilt, fear, prioritizing the feelings or perceptions of others... When I recognized these incongruencies, I was able to address them and do the work that actually dropped the energetic block. Recognize the block, if you can, and then see it falling away. Over and over again until you really feel, in the deep part of your heart, that it is no longer there.

Work to re-program your personal beliefs. Remind yourself that having what you want only creates more of it – more of you – to give to others, however you choose. Remind yourself that you deserve it. Tell yourself why you deserve it – you're amazing, that's why! You share yourself with others, that's why! You share your wealth, that's why! You respect and love others, that's why!

Train your brain to think of your issue in a new and positive way, and then feel the good – ALL. THE. GOOD. Your success in whatever you are working to manifest, will come.

Feel the 'different' version. Perhaps you aren't manifesting what you want because you can't really imagine yourself having it. Practice seeing yourself, FEELING yourself, with the thing you want to create. Imagine how it will change you, imagine how you will feel after that change, after this thing comes into your life. Practice talking about it as if it's already happened. Practice celebrating its arrival.

Last, be patient. There is a danger in wanting something too much. The underlying message in "I want it" is "I still don't have it." Go back to gratitude. FEEL yourself already having it. And then accept that when you aren't getting what you think you want, there may be a reason. You are where you are meant to be. Look for the lesson. And then surrender, trusting your soul-self.

Keep working, of course. Keep loving yourself first and ever more deeply. Keep visualizing. Keep honing your own energy and connecting more perfectly to the god self, the soul self within. Keep repeating your mantra. And be patient. Time is an illusion we all subscribe to and understanding that energy is irrespective of time will help. Believe your 'thing' is coming. Because it is. Keep doing your work. Keep creating. Keep trusting. Be patient.

And LOVE YOUR MAGICAL SELF!

www.ingramcontent.com/pod-product-compliance
Lightning Source LLC
Chambersburg PA
CBHW061832040426
42447CB00012B/2927